THE LOCAL CHURCH

JOHN SIEBELING

JOHNSIEBELING
JOHNSIEBELING.COM

The Local Church

Request for information should be addressed to:

John Siebeling Ministries, 650 Houston Hill Road, Eads, TN 38028

ISBN-13: 978-1-956383-01-0

Printed in the United States of America.

johnsiebeling.com

CONTENTS

INTRODUCTION

"The righteous will flourish like a palm tree, they will grow like a cedar of Lebanon; planted in the house of the Lord, they will flourish in the courts of our God" (Psalm 92:12–13).

For the majority of my life, this has been a defining passage of Scripture for me. I remember the special season when I gave my life to Jesus as a young man and found my place in God's House. Looking back, I can confidently say planting myself in a local church and devoting my life to building God's House has been one of the greatest decisions I have made. I have experienced firsthand what this verse describes: a life that's flourishing and thriving—not because of me, but because of the blessing, protection and favor that comes from being planted in the House of the Lord.

Throughout this book, we will explore what the Bible says about the local church, what a healthy church looks like, what it means to be planted and the benefits it brings into our lives and so much more.

The church is such a powerful and purposeful part of God's plan. I hope you'll keep your heart open as we dive in and discover all the amazing things God has for us in His House!

GOD'S HOUSE, GOD'S IDEA

GOD'S HOUSE, GOD'S IDEA

"At the center of all this, Christ rules the church. The church, you see, is not peripheral to the world; the world is peripheral to the church. The church is Christ's body, in which he speaks and acts, by which he fills everything with his presence"
(Ephesians 1:22-23 MSG).

The church is a central part of God's blueprint for how His people live and thrive, both individually and corporately. It's also part of His plan for how a broken and hurting world receives the hope it so desperately needs.

We would all agree that blueprints are an essential component when building a house. And when we realize the church is part of God's blueprint for our spiritual lives and for reaching the world, we can see just how important it is.

The local church exists through people, in a place, for a purpose.

When you make a decision to follow Jesus and you give Him your life, some powerful things take place! First, you're forgiven of your sin and your past. How amazing! That decision changes the trajectory of your life. Not only are you forgiven of your past, but you have a whole new future. The Bible says you become a brand new person (2 Corinthians 5:17 NLT).

Secondly, you are "spiritually" transferred from the kingdom of darkness into the kingdom of God (Colossians 1:13 NLT). Part of that transfer is that you automatically become a member of *The Church*—"Capital C"—the great body of believers around the world who are following Jesus. How amazing to be part of the great movement of God's living, breathing, growing church!

But there's more to God's plan for you than just being part of the global church at large. As a Christian, one of the most important spiritual decisions you can make is to find a local church and get planted. We need to find a *local expression* of that "Capital C" Church—a local church that you can be part of.

Ephesians 2:19 gives us a great picture of this: *"Now you are no longer strangers to God and foreigners to heaven, but* ***you are members of God's very own family****, citizens of God's country, and you* ***belong in God's household*** *with every other Christian"* (TLB, emphasis mine).

Here we see the intended progression God designed to take place:

"...you are members of God's very own family..." We become a Christian, and when we do, we become part of the worldwide body of believers.

"...you belong in God's household..." Being a part of the family isn't enough; after we become a Christian, we need to find a local church home—a place to belong.

God's design is that these two both take place and that every person who joins the family of God also finds a place in the *household* of God.

From Genesis to Revelation, God has always worked through people and placed those people in specific settings. In the Old Testament, He led His people to build the Tabernacle, a portable tent of worship where His presence would dwell. Later, Solomon built the Temple in Jerusalem, an awe-inspiring structure filled with beauty, detail and reverence.

These weren't just construction projects. They were God's chosen places to meet with His people. Worship happened there. Community happened there.

Forgiveness, sacrifice and blessing all flowed from those places.

In fact, Psalm 26:8 says *"Lord, I love the house where you live, the place where your glory dwells."*

God's presence was tangible in the House. Today, we don't need a temple made of stone. We are the temple of the Holy Spirit. But that doesn't mean that a place doesn't matter. God still gathers His people together in churches, buildings and communities. His presence still meets us there. We gather as the church. And when we gather in His name, God shows up (Matthew 18:20).

Why Is the Church So Important?

To put it simply, the church should matter to us because it matters to God. Throughout Scripture, we see the church described using powerful metaphors loaded with spiritual meaning:

The Body of Christ—*"He makes the whole body fit together perfectly. As each part does its own special work, it helps the other parts grow..."* (Ephesians 4:16 NLT).

As a Christian, you're part of something larger than

yourself. There is a place for you! The gifts and talents God created in you help the other parts grow and make the whole better.

The Bride of Christ—*"...Christ loved the church and gave himself up for her"* (Ephesians 5:25).

Here we see the incredible love that Jesus has for the church—a love so great He was willing to give His life for her. If the church matters that much to Jesus, it should matter that much to us, too.

The House of God—*"...God's household, which is the church of the living God, the pillar and foundation of the truth"* (1 Timothy 3:15).

This shows us the church as the foundational place of truth and strength. It speaks to the steadfastness that can anchor us when life is uncertain.

These metaphors show us not only the value God places on the church and the great love He has for it, but they also show us the incredible gift the church is to us.

The church is not an afterthought to God, and it shouldn't be to us either. It's not just a gathering or a spiritual idea. It's a divine reality with impact that is both supernatural and practical.

It's **the Body**, where every believer has a place to belong and a part to play. It's **the Bride**, deeply loved and cherished by Jesus. And it's **the House**, built with order, strength and spiritual authority, providing a home and a place of safety for those who are in it.

The Church Is Essential

We live in a world full of options. We can customize everything from our coffee to our playlists and convenience often shapes our commitments. It's easy to carry that same mindset into our faith, treating church as something we attend when it fits our schedule. But God never designed the church to be optional. He created it to be essential for our growth, our protection and our purpose.

Hebrews 10:25 reminds us, *"Let us not neglect our church meetings, as some people do, but encourage and warn each other, especially now that the day of his coming back again is drawing near"* (TLB).

The church is God's idea. Now more than ever, we need the church, and the world needs the church. It's part of God's plan for you and for the world we live in, and it has been since the beginning of time.

The Church Is Still God's Plan

There's been a growing idea in our culture that you can love God without loving the church. That church is optional and your faith can thrive privately as long as you read your Bible and listen to worship and teaching. Those things are important, but they were never meant to replace the holistic experience of having a life that is planted in a local church.

The truth is that the church is not a trend or an earthly movement. It's not a human invention; it's a divine institution. The church was birthed in the heart of God long before it was built on earth. And that is what makes it so powerful and significant.

Jesus said, *"...I will build my church, and all the powers of hell will not conquer it"* (Matthew 16:18 NLT).

That single phrase—*my church*—says everything. Jesus didn't say a church or some church. He said, my church. This shows ownership. Authority. Vision. These things came straight from the mouth of Jesus Himself, about the church.

When we talk about being a part of the church, we're talking about participating in the very thing Jesus is building on the earth.

"All this energy issues from Christ: God raised him from death and set him on a throne in deep heaven, in charge of running the universe, everything from galaxies to governments, no name and no power exempt from his rule. And not just for the time being, but forever. He is in charge of it all, has the final word on everything. At the center of all this, Christ rules the church. The church, you see, is not peripheral to the world; the world is peripheral to the church. The church is Christ's body, in which he speaks and acts, by which he fills everything with his presence" (Ephesians 1:20–23 MSG).

Here's what makes it even more beautiful. The church is not just global; it's local. It's a huge family that spans the globe, and yet, there is a place for you and me right where we are. Because, as I said before, we need the church and the church needs us.

There can be a temptation to label the church as old-fashioned or flawed and use that as an excuse to dismiss it. People say things like, "I love Jesus, I just don't like organized religion," or "I do church on my own," or "The church hurt me."

The church may not be perfect. Churches are made up of people, and we all know that people are imperfect. Unfortunately, I've seen the dysfunction. I've experienced the disappointment. But even still, I'm all in. And my life is so much richer for it. I'm so glad I didn't cut and run when it hurt or when things got tough.

Yes, it's messy. But it's also miraculous. It is the thing Jesus is building. And it's the only place on earth where people from every background, race, story and season can gather in unity under one name: the name of Jesus.

Some have compared the church to Noah's Ark. It wasn't perfect. Imagine the smell, the mess, the noise, the cramped quarters. But it was the only thing floating in a global flood. It was God's provision for salvation in a time of judgment.

The same is true for the church. It may not always be neat and tidy. Sometimes things get messy. It's not always comfortable. But when the storms of life hit or when culture is flooded with confusion, compromise and chaos, the church is still God's rescue plan. It always has been and it always will be, and we get to be part of it.

God's House, Your Home

Maybe you've never been committed to a church. Maybe you've bounced around churches. Maybe you've been hurt. Maybe you've been burned out or disappointed. I know those experiences are painful, and you may be reluctant to open back up to the idea of church. Churches are made up of imperfect people, so there will never be a perfect one, but you can find one that is doing its best to honor God and love people well.

I love what Eugene Peterson says in his book, *The Pastor: A Memoir:* "Congregation is composed of people, who, upon entering a church, leave behind what people on the street name or call them. A church can never be reduced to a place where goods and services are exchanged. It must never be a place where a person is labeled. It can never be a place where gossip is perpetuated. Before anything else, it is a place where a person is named and greeted, whether implicitly or explicitly, in Jesus's name. A place where dignity is conferred."[1]

If church has been a place you've drifted away from or avoided, can I extend an invitation to you today? Give the church another chance.

Ask God to show you the local church He's calling you to and then go all in. If you've been waiting for the perfect church, let me remind you: it doesn't exist. Even if it did, it wouldn't be perfect once we walked through the door.

The church isn't a crowd. It's a community and a spiritual family. You were made for belonging, for a home. And one of the places where you can find that is a healthy local church.

Action Steps

- **If you don't have a local church home, ask God to help you find the church that's right for you.** Attend a service with the intention of seeking God's leading with an open, surrendered heart.

- **If you do have a local church, think about what it means to be planted.** Ask yourself, *Am I truly planted in the way that God's Word describes?*

- **Take one step closer to community and connection.** That might be choosing to attend a service if you haven't been in church. If you do have a church, maybe it's introducing yourself to someone new, filling out a prayer request card for a need you're facing or joining a small group or serve team.

Reflection Questions

1. What has been your personal experience with church—positive, negative or mixed? How has that shaped your view of the local church today?

2. Do you see the local church as essential or optional in your life right now? What influenced that belief?

3. Is there anything that has kept you from planting yourself in a local church? What might God be inviting you to surrender or rethink?

GOD'S DIVINE DESIGN FOR THE CHURCH

GOD'S DIVINE DESIGN FOR THE CHURCH

"...I will put together my church, a church so expansive with energy that not even the gates of hell will be able to keep it out" (Matthew 16:18 MSG).

A few years ago, I walked by a church in downtown Boston, Massachusetts, that has been meeting for more than 350 years. Think about that. Through every major American event including wars, economic collapses, civil rights battles and cultural shifts, the church has stood.

It's not just in the United States. Around the world, in nations like Iran, China and North Korea, the church is growing under intense persecution. In places where it's illegal to preach, believers are worshiping in secret, building community underground and seeing salvations every day.

In fact, Daniel prophesied about this unshakable kingdom: *"During the reigns of those kings, the God of heaven will set up a kingdom that will never be destroyed or conquered...and it will stand forever"* (Daniel 2:44 NLT).

That kingdom he spoke about? That's the church.

Tried, Tested and Triumphant

If you watch the news or listen to commentators, some people say we're living in the worst time in history. I'm not so sure. No doubt we are living in challenging times. But, amazingly, the church has endured far more than what we're seeing today. Political division? Global pandemics? Social upheaval? The church has outlasted empires, endured plagues and survived revolutions, persecution and wars. Not only has the church survived, *it has come out on the other side tried, tested and triumphant. And it will continue to*. This is what Jesus promised: not even the gates of hell will be able to stop it or take it out.

The victorious nature of the church is ultimately rooted in God's supreme power. But He's also called us into partnership with Him to build His church here on earth. So, if we want to understand what the "secret" to the lasting power and triumph of the church has been, we have to go back to the beginning and see how God designed the church in its original form.

When we do this, we see the picture of a church that was born to make a difference. Not to be passive or secondary to the culture it was in, or something easy to ignore. In fact, when we look at the birth of the church in Acts, we see just the opposite.

Since its inception, the church has carried a supernatural power that was not contained by the chaos and turbulence of the world it came into. In fact, the power of the church was so strong that it created a divine disruption of the cultural chaos and spiritual complacency of the day. Offering something different—something that could not be ignored!

When we look at the picture of the church and the impact that it's having around the world, we see that it is a force to be reckoned with. In every season, it may be tried and tested, but it continues to emerge triumphant. And that's because it's something God designed, and there isn't a power that can stand against it.

A Church in Motion

One of the things I love about the Book of Acts is how it shows the church in motion. It was dynamic. It was a wildfire of faith that couldn't be contained.

"When the day of Pentecost came, they were all together in one place. Suddenly a sound like the blowing of a violent wind came from heaven...They saw what seemed to be tongues of fire that separated

and came to rest on each of them. All of them were filled with the Holy Spirit..." (Acts 2:1–4).

That wasn't a quiet beginning. The disciples, a group numbering around 120 people (Acts 1:15), are praying in a place called the Upper Room (Acts 1:13) and suddenly, there's an eruption of something supernatural that arrives on the scene—a divine disruption. The wind of the Holy Spirit comes from heaven, fire falls and they are all filled with the Holy Spirit. In all the holy commotion, a curious crowd gathers to try to understand what is happening (Acts 2:6). Peter stands up and preaches and about 3,000 people surrender their lives to Jesus and join in with them. Wow! In just a few hours, the 120 in the Upper Room grew to 3,120 people! The church is born!

In Acts 1:8, the promise had been given when Jesus told the disciples before His ascension: *"But you will receive power when the Holy Spirit comes on you; and you will be my witnesses in Jerusalem, and in all Judea and Samaria, and to the ends of the earth."* Acts 1:8 is often called the "programmatic verse" of the Book of Acts because it outlines the whole trajectory of the story. This wasn't just a command from Jesus; it was a roadmap.

The rest of Acts unfolds exactly in that pattern: the church is born and grows in Jerusalem (Acts 1-7), persecution drives believers into Judea and Samaria (Acts 8–12) and through Paul's missionary journeys, the gospel reaches the ends of the earth, culminating in Rome (Acts 13–28).

Pentecost (Acts 2) is the beginning of that fulfillment. The Spirit empowers the disciples to witness in Jerusalem, but it's only the first step in the bigger story. The importance of Acts 1:8 is that it keeps us from viewing Pentecost as a one-time event for one group.

Instead, it frames the entire book as the Spirit's ongoing work to carry the message of Jesus outward in widening circles. In this sense, Acts 1:8 is a mission statement for the early church: the Spirit empowers the church for a global witness, beginning locally and moving outward to every nation.

I believe this is a pattern for how the Church is supposed to operate *today.* It's what we pray for, lead toward and build into the fabric of our modern-day churches. Years ago, when I was in Bible school, one of my teachers taught us a principle called The Law of First Mention. The principle suggests that the first time a particular word, concept or doctrine appears in the Scriptures establishes its foundational meaning. If we want to know why the church was born in the first place, let's look at the Book of Acts so we can truly understand what God intended church to be and then go build the church Jesus had in mind when He gave His life on the cross.

12 Characteristics of the Local Church

I believe the local church we read about in Acts represents an example and a pattern for us today. Patterns are important. My mom liked to sew. I can remember her pulling out her sewing machine and taking patterns and cutting out fabric, sewing dresses for my sisters. Every project she would sew always started with a pattern.

Let's look at this pattern we see in the Book of Acts. In it, we see **12 specific characteristics of the early church.** If the church was a recipe, it would have 12 ingredients. Twelve qualities necessary for the church to be the church. Some of these are tasks, some we can measure easily and others are more intangible. As I list them out, refer back to this foundational passage:

"They devoted themselves to the apostles' teaching and to fellowship, to the breaking of bread and to

prayer. Everyone was filled with awe at the many wonders and signs performed by the apostles. All the believers were together and had everything in common. They sold property and possessions to give to anyone who had need. Every day they continued to meet together in the temple courts. They broke bread in their homes and ate together with glad and sincere hearts, praising God and enjoying the favor of all the people. And the Lord added to their number daily those who were being saved" (Acts 2:42–47).

1. Devotion Is a Hallmark

"They devoted themselves."

Everyone pressed into God individually. I wouldn't say any of these are in any order of importance, but this first one is what holds all the others together. There was a sense of devotion in the early believers. Church wasn't a duty or an obligation. They wanted to be there! The Oxford Dictionary defines devotion as *love, loyalty, or enthusiasm for a person, activity or cause* (emphasis mine). What's in our hearts and the motivation behind our actions matter. When our heart is aligned with what matters to God, that devotion and commitment are catalysts that will multiply our spiritual growth.

This wasn't casual Christianity. This wasn't convenient faith. It was intentional, sacrificial, joyful devotion. They were all in.

"Never be lacking in zeal, but keep your spiritual fervor, serving the Lord" (Romans 12:11).

In today's world, devotion looks like showing up even when it's inconvenient, staying rooted when things get hard and serving without needing attention or recognition. A church full of devoted people is a church that's dangerous to darkness.

2. God's Word Is Central

"They devoted themselves to the apostles' teaching."

God's Word was their foundation, and it is still the foundation for all we do. We love God's Word. When God's Word is central in the life of a church, the believers there will have a sure foundation for their future.

We need to read God's Word personally and sit under the anointed teaching of God's Word in church. It all matters!

"All Scripture is God-breathed and is useful for teaching, rebuking, correcting and training in righteousness" (2 Timothy 3:16).

In a time when culture is constantly shifting, we need truth that never changes. The early church was built on what the apostles taught, which was the gospel of Jesus and the Scriptures they'd grown up on. We do the same today. Churches with a weak grip on the Word produce weak believers. But churches that love the Bible—teach it, apply it, live it—raise up disciples who can stand through anything.

3. Community Is the Glue

"They devoted themselves to...fellowship."

There is an important word in this passage that we don't hear very often these days: fellowship. In the original language, it is the Greek word "koinonia", which describes the relationship between these believers as special. They had a unique family bond because of their shared relationship with Christ. They were all part of this new family. The family of God!

There is an important call to action in this passage because of this word—a compelling call that we are supposed to be together as believers, together as family, together as His Church.

"By this everyone will know that you are my disciples, if you love one another" (John 13:35).

They didn't just attend together. They shared meals, needs, moments and mission. This is why finding connection in small groups is so important. Church is not just rows—it's circles. And the more we grow relationally, the stronger we become spiritually.

4. Prayer Is Vital

"They devoted themselves to...prayer."

The power of prayer! They prayed for each other. They prayed for the church! They prayed personally. They prayed corporately. Prayer is not a last resort but a first response.

I personally believe prayer is central to the health and vitality of a local church. Praying together in weekend services and special times of prayer throughout the year is transformative.

"...they raised their voices together in prayer to God" (Acts 4:24).

"The prayer of a righteous person is powerful and effective" (James 5:16).

Prayer keeps our hearts soft and our vision clear. The early church knew they couldn't do anything in their own strength. That hasn't changed. We don't grow the church through personality, creativity or strategy alone. We grow it through prayer-powered obedience to the Spirit.

5. The Fear of God Creates the Atmosphere

"Everyone was filled with awe..."

There was a reverential fear of the Lord. The fear of the Lord is a theme throughout Scripture. It doesn't mean terror. It means honor and respect. They had a respect for God and the things of God. The respect and honor opened the door for God to move in their lives.

"The fear of the Lord is the beginning of wisdom..." (Proverbs 9:10).

"The Lord confides in those who fear him..." (Psalm 25:14).

We need to reclaim holy awe in our churches. Not a stiff, religious spirit but a humble awareness that God is in the room. That we're not just attending something, but we're meeting with Someone.

Where there's honor, there's presence. And where there's presence, there's power.

6. Miracles Are Present

"...many wonders and signs..."

The healing power of God was present. There were miracles and signs and wonders. This carries over from the ministry of Jesus. He told the disciples (and us today) that we would do even greater things than He did because He was going to heaven and sending the Holy Spirit (John 14:12).

Our churches today need to be environments of great faith where we can see and sense the power and presence of God.

"And these signs will accompany those who believe..." (Mark 16:17).

"Very truly I tell you, whoever believes in me will do the works I have been doing..." (John 14:12).

We don't manufacture the miraculous, but we *make room for it.* In our teaching, our worship, our prayers. The early church didn't treat miracles as rare. They expected them. And when we walk in unity, humility and boldness—we can too.

7. Generosity Is a Lifestyle

"...to give..."

Financial generosity was a part of church life from the very beginning. It is a part of our spiritual DNA to invest financially so the church can fulfill its mission. Generosity keeps the gas tank full and the vehicle moving forward!

The generosity of the early church wasn't forced. It was voluntary, joyful and sacrificial. They gave to meet needs. They gave to sustain the mission. They gave because they understood that everything they had belonged to God anyway.

"Each of you should give what you have decided in your heart to give, not reluctantly or under compulsion, for God loves a cheerful giver" (2 Corinthians 9:7).

"Bring the whole tithe into the storehouse, that there may be food in my house..." (Malachi 3:10).

Giving is not just a financial act—it's a spiritual discipline. It breaks the grip of materialism and expands our impact. A generous church is a powerful church, because generosity fuels ministry.

8. Those in Need Are Served

"...to anyone who had need."

A major role of the church is serving those in need. As churches, we are planted in communities to make those communities better and serve the underserved.

The early church didn't ignore need. They responded to it. The text tells us they sold possessions and shared resources to care for one another. That's radical generosity. That's love in action.

"If anyone has material possessions and sees a brother or sister in need but has no pity on them, how can the love of God be in that person?" (1 John 3:17).

"Religion that God our Father accepts as pure and faultless is this: to look after orphans and widows in their distress..." (James 1:27).

Churches are not spiritual bunkers. We are beacons of hope. And part of our mission is to bring practical help to people in crisis, pain or poverty. When the church rises to meet real-world needs, it shows the love of Jesus in undeniable ways.

9. Worship Services Are a Priority

"...continued to meet together in the temple courts."

This new church met as a congregation at the Temple in Jerusalem at a place called Solomon's Portico (or Solomon's Colonnade or Solomon's Porch). It was a massive outdoor area on the eastern side of the Temple that held thousands upon thousands of people.

The church grew throughout the Book of Acts from approximately 120 in the Upper Room (Acts 1:15) to approximately 3,120 on the day of Pentecost (Acts 2:41). Another number is mentioned in Acts 4:4, where it says that the number of men came to be about 5,000. If you add in women and children, the church in Jerusalem—the first church—could easily have been 15,000 to 25,000 people.

And they all met together and worshiped together in large, powerful worship services.

The pattern for the church has always included public celebration services. Scripture also says they broke bread in their homes and ate together. This combination of large and small environments enabled these new believers (and you and me today) to experience all the benefits of church life.

"I rejoiced with those who said to me, 'Let us go to the house of the Lord'" (Psalm 122:1).

"Every day they continued to meet together in the temple courts..." (Acts 2:46).

Church isn't optional—it's essential. And when the people of God gather to worship in unity, heaven moves. Something happens in the room that can't happen in isolation.

10. Joy Is Evident

"...praising God and enjoying..."

I love this one. These new believers were enjoying their new life in Christ and in church. There is joy in the presence of God! I wholeheartedly believe church is meant to be enjoyed and not endured.

"You make known to me the path of life; you will fill me with joy in your presence..." (Psalm 16:11).

"...the joy of the Lord is your strength" (Nehemiah 8:10).

Joy is a Fruit of the Spirit (Galatians 5:22), and it should be one of the most tangible marks of our church gatherings. Not fake smiles or hype but real, deep, contagious joy that flows from people who know they're saved, loved and planted in God's House.

A joyless church is not a healthy church. But a joyful church? It's magnetic. People want to be part of it. They're drawn to the life that joy brings.

11. Favor Is Enjoyed

"...enjoying the favor..."

They walked in and enjoyed the favor of God and people! At one point in the Book of Acts, it says the people held them in high esteem.

"No one else dared join them, even though they were highly regarded by the people" (Acts 5:13).

"Surely, Lord, you bless the righteous; you surround them with your favor as with a shield" (Psalm 5:12).

Favor isn't something we can earn or manufacture. It's a gift from God that comes through obedience and alignment with His will.

The early church wasn't perfect, but they walked in unity, holiness and generosity. And because of that, the outside world noticed. They gained credibility and influence not by compromising, but by *living authentically.*

Churches that walk in health often find that favor follows. Open doors. Community partnerships. Unexplainable growth. Strategic influence. God gives favor to churches that honor Him.

12. The Lost Are Found

"And the Lord added to their number daily those who were being saved."

One of the most important qualities of church life is welcoming the lost home.

The word "lost" is used by Jesus to describe those outside of God's family, a spiritual state of disconnection from God. In fact, Jesus gave us His ultimate mission in Luke 19:10, *"For the Son of Man came to seek and to save the lost."*

This is why it must always be part of our mission as a church to give people the opportunity to repent of their sin and surrender their lives to Jesus. Salvation! The early church wasn't just growing by transfer. They were growing by conversion. People were meeting

Jesus every day. Why? Because the church was alive, visible, compelling and faithful to the message.

Evangelism is not a department in the church. It is the heartbeat of the church.

"For 'Everyone who calls on the name of the Lord will be saved.'...And how can they hear about him unless someone tells them?" (Romans 10:13–14 NLT).

When churches lose their passion for the lost, they lose their purpose. We are here to reach people. Period.

When you're planted in a local church, you're not just filling a seat; you're fulfilling a mission. You're part of God's global church, the body of Christ that is bringing light into dark places and calling people home to Him. Together, we help others find hope, freedom and new life in Jesus. There is nothing else on earth like the church, and nothing more powerful than a believer who knows what they're a part of.

Finding the Right Local Church for You

I believe it is really important to find the right local church for you. There's no such thing as a perfect church because churches are filled with imperfect people. But there is a right place for you to plant yourself. I believe God has a local church for you. It may take a season to find it, but you need to find it. And as you do, you will feel a grace come into your life for that place, that local church. I know you're thinking—what does that mean? It's a little hard to describe, but it's just a sense that you will have a "knowing in your heart" that it is the right place for you.

When I was in college, I had a few struggles in my personal life and I thought maybe I needed to find a different church. A new place where I could just kind of start over in my faith journey. So, I started trying out some Bible studies and services at another church. They were great, but I felt like a fish out of water. The worship was pretty much the same and the church's beliefs were exactly the same. And yet, I felt awkward and out of place. Why? Because I wasn't graced for that place.

We can't base choosing a church completely on our feelings and whether or not we feel comfortable there. The reality is, especially at first, the church I was graced for did make me uncomfortable! But it was in the right ways. God was pulling me out of my comfort zone spiritually, and deep down, I still sensed it was where I belonged. Having that experience ended up being a good test for me. It confirmed where I needed to be and those I needed to be with.

This chapter offers a glimpse into what a healthy, life-giving church looks like. One that reflects God's original design from the Book of Acts and still thrives in our world today. The church was never meant to be a static institution; it is a living, breathing expression of Christ on earth—His hands, His heart and His hope for the world. When we find a local church that embodies these characteristics, we find a place where faith grows, lives are changed and the gospel moves forward.

In the coming chapters, we'll explore what it means to become part of a local church in a meaningful way: the spiritual and practical steps of planting yourself deeply, the blessings that come from belonging and how being rooted in God's House positions you to flourish in every area of life.

Action Steps

- **Identify the next step that you need to take toward getting planted.** If you don't have a church, maybe it's setting aside time to research local options or sending a text to someone who might be able to give you some recommendations.

- **If you are connected to a healthy local church, look for ways you can contribute** to helping your church embody the characteristics God designed the church to display. Be generous, look for opportunities to welcome those who don't know Jesus, make attending services a priority in your life—whatever is on that list, ask God where you can be a part of making it possible in your church.

Reflection Questions

1. Which of the twelve characteristics of the early church (devotion, teaching, fellowship, prayer, awe, miracles, serving, generosity, worship, joy, favor, reaching the lost) stands out most to you personally? Why?

2. The early believers were described as "devoted." What does devotion look like for you in this season?

PLANTED IN THE HOUSE OF THE LORD

PLANTED IN THE HOUSE OF THE LORD

"The righteous will flourish like a palm tree, they will grow like a cedar of Lebanon; planted in the house of the Lord, they will flourish in the courts of our God" (Psalm 92:12–13).

In the first chapter, we talked about why the local church matters—how God sees it, how important it is to Him and why it should be important to us. In the previous chapter, we talked about the birth of the local church—the characteristics God designed the local church to have, how the church is God's rescue plan for the world and how we have a part to play in it.

What an incredible thought it is that our lives can be part of something larger than ourselves on such a significant level. We can be part of bringing hope and salvation to a hurting world and leave a legacy that carries eternal impact!

That brings us to an important question: *How do I create a meaningful connection with a local church that allows me to experience the benefits of God's intended plan in my own life and be part of bringing God's rescue plan to others?*

It starts with being planted in a healthy local church.

As I mentioned at the beginning of the book, Psalm 92:12–13 has been one of the themes of my life, and it's a verse that I've seen to be true year after year. My life has flourished because I have planted myself in God's House.

Good Things in God's House

I don't think there's anyone in the Bible who expressed a greater love for God's House than David. When you read the Book of Psalms, which is really like David's diary, his commitment to God's House is evident. David says in Psalm 23:6, *"I will dwell in the house of the Lord forever."*

Many of these Psalms weren't written with the intention for us to read; they were simply David pouring out his deepest thoughts and emotions. The Bible calls David a man after God's own heart (1 Samuel 13:14), and now thousands of years later, we have the benefit of looking at what was in his heart concerning the House of God.

When we read about David, we see that church was a huge part of his life. He was incredibly passionate about it. Some people might look at these passages about God's House and wonder if this is still relevant for our lives in this day and age. The answer is yes! A commitment and love for God's House today carries the same significance and benefits that it always has.

Here are some of the things the Bible tells us we experience when we're planted in a healthy local church:

God's Presence

Psalm 26:8—*"I love your sanctuary, Lord,* ***the place where your glorious presence dwells****"* (NLT, emphasis mine).

God's Protection

Psalm 27:4-5—"*One thing I ask from the Lord, this only do I seek: that I may dwell in the house of the Lord all the days of my life...****For in the day of trouble he will keep me safe in his dwelling****; he will hide me in the shelter of his sacred tent and set me high upon a rock*" (emphasis mine).

God's Provision

Psalm 65:4—"*We are filled with the good things of your house...*"

Psalm 36:8—*"They feast on the abundance of your house..."*

Some of the "good things" we experience in God's House:

- Relationships
- An opportunity to make a difference
- Encouragement and support
- Spiritual growth
- Purpose

As we can see from these verses, God's House is full of benefits for our lives. How do we receive all the benefits of God's House in our lives? By being planted!

What Does It Mean to Be Planted?

To be planted means *to set in the soil for growth; to set firmly in position; to establish; to fix firmly.* The analogy here is the analogy of a garden or a field. Your life is like a seed and the local church is like the ground or the soil. **God wants you to be planted in the local church for your spiritual growth!**

Without the seed, the soil is pretty much insignificant. Without the soil, the seed is fairly insignificant as well. But together they can produce a crop that can be enjoyed, even used to produce more crops! It is when they come together that they produce something significant. The same is true about our lives and the local church. When we plant ourselves in the local church, it produces something beautiful, productive, even powerful and influential.

How does it work? The seed has all of the potential. The life isn't in the soil; the life is in the seed. The seed cannot bring out all of that potential that's inside of it. Only the soil has the ability to draw that life out of the seed. Without the soil, the life that is inside the seed cannot be initiated or sustained.

Within every seed there is life, an embryo, and covering the embryo is the outer wall of the seed.

The key to starting the process of growth and germination is impacting that outer wall. Something has to touch that outer wall. In most seeds, it's a combination of three things that initiate life—warmth, light and moisture.

The important thing about the soil is that it has to:

- Be **strong enough** to hold the seed in place.
- Be **flexible enough** to allow the roots to push through the bottom and the buds to sprout from the top.
- Be **healthy enough** to provide the seed with the right environment for growth.

Think about the spiritual analogy and how that applies to our lives:

The seed represents me and you. We are the seeds, packed with potential and life. God puts it inside of us. He also gives us a divinely implanted sense of purpose. Deep in the core of our being, we yearn to be significant and make a difference with our lives. That sense of significance is put within us by God.

The soil represents the environment and atmosphere of the local church. A healthy local church is strong enough to hold us in place, and flexible enough to allow us to deepen our roots, bud and blossom. Remember, the soil holds the seed and is what allows it to have sustained growth. It's also the source of the key ingredients that are necessary for growth.

Just like the soil provides the seed with what it needs to grow, a healthy local church provides us with what we need to grow and mature as believers: God's presence, His Word, good relationships, the Holy Spirit and more. In the same way that a seed needs soil in order to grow and produce fruit, we need a local church to grow and become all God wants us to be.

Planted: So Much More Than Just Attending

Think about the seed of a tree, planted into the soil. After it's planted, it begins to grow. As growth takes place, its roots go deep. It weathers storms. It grows in every season. Over time, it becomes something strong, something fruitful, something that lasts.

This is the picture that we see depicted in God's Word when it comes to how God intends for our lives to relate to the local church. This is when we experience the fullness of all He intended it to be.

But here's what's really important: we can't be planted if we don't stay committed and consistent in one place. In order to experience the benefits of flourishing, we need to start by making sure we're attending church regularly. But that's just getting us to the starting line of what God is inviting us to experience with church. He's calling us to be *planted.*

There is a key distinction that I think so many people miss, and as a result, they don't experience church as God intended it to be. Being *planted* in church is so much more than *attending* a church; it's when your life is rooted in it.

Attending is showing up when it's convenient; planted

is building your life around it. Attending is being there and checking a box; planted is being present, heart and soul. Attending is kind of like autopilot. You can attend and be there in body but not in spirit.

The word "planted", on the other hand, is intentional. It speaks to stability. Longevity. Connectedness. It is being all in and anchored. When you're connected and anchored to something, it's not something you show up for and then go back to your life; it's the lifeblood that everything else flows from. It's commitment and consistency. Being all in, even when it's not easy or convenient. This is not a concept our culture tends to gravitate toward. But when it comes to our spiritual lives, transformation happens through commitment.

There's a mindset shift that happens when someone goes from just attending church to *being planted* in church. They begin to move from just being an attender to becoming a contributor.

An attender asks, *What do I get from this church?* A contributor asks, *What can I contribute to this church?*

You were designed by God for a life of community, serving, blessing others and building what Jesus is building—the church. We'll talk later about how powerful this is in our lives, but for now, I just want to remind you that God has created you with purpose and there are good things He created you to do.

"For we are God's handiwork, created in Christ Jesus to do good works, which God prepared in advance for us to do" (Ephesians 2:10).

This verse doesn't say, "prepared in advance for pastors to do." It says us. All of us. Every believer has a part to play. When we each do our part, the whole body grows. You were created with unique gifts and talents to make a difference and contribute to what God is doing! When you engage with what God is building, you not only experience the growth God designed us to experience, but you also help create a place where others experience growth too. What an incredible thing to think about. There's no better place to invest our gifts and talents than into something that will impact people's lives in a way that can last for eternity!

What Do Planted People Do?

Let's talk practically for a moment. If being planted is the goal, what does that look like? What do planted people actually do?

Let me give you five simple, practical steps:

1. **They show up consistently.** Not just when it's easy. Every week, in every season, they prioritize the House of God.
2. **They engage in worship.** Planted people don't spectate, they participate. They come early to church so they're ready to worship. They're leaning in during the service.
3. **They serve on a team.** They find their place in God's House and give back. Whether it's holding a door open and welcoming people or leading a small group, they're in it.
4. **They give financially.** Planted people tithe. They sow into the vision. They trust God with their finances.
5. **They build relationships.** They go beyond just showing up at the weekly services and establish community in their church. They make time for small groups.

This isn't about checking boxes. It's about investing in the soil where you're planted. When you're planted, it impacts you, but you also make the church stronger for others. Your presence encourages. Your service strengthens. Your giving fuels the vision. You're not just growing yourself. You're helping others grow, too.

Consistency Builds Strength

As you stay planted, spiritual consistency begins to grow in your life. Like an oak tree that is slow growing, deeply rooted and weather resistant.

"But blessed is the one who trusts in the Lord... They will be like a tree planted by the water... It does not fear when heat comes; its leaves are always green. It has no worries in a year of drought and never fails to bear fruit" (Jeremiah 17:7–8).

That's the promise of being planted. Not a storm-free life, but a storm-proof life. Your roots go down, and you grow through seasons, whether good or bad.

I've seen families in our church who've stayed planted through personal tragedy—the death of a loved one, the loss of a dream job, disappointment. They didn't uproot; they dug deeper. They leaned into God and they leaned into their church family. Years later, they're still standing. Still serving. Still bearing fruit. That's what being planted looks like.

Barriers to Being Planted

A lot of times I hear people say they want to be more involved in church, but there are so many reasons why they can't. Let's be honest: life is full and there are always things that are going to pull at our attention, time, finances and focus. The truth is, we make time for what matters to us. It may be true that your schedule right now doesn't allow for the bandwidth to be planted. I would challenge you if that's the case to look at your priorities and what will bring true, lasting value to your life and build the legacy you want to leave one day.

If the life you have now doesn't reflect that and if your current priorities don't leave room at the top for church, I encourage you to make a change. There is nothing that can replace being planted in God's House. It's what He's called us to, and it's what our lives need.

Let me speak to a few of the common things that keep people from being planted:

1. Busyness

Life is full. Work, family, school, sports, travel, errands. I could keep going. We live in a time where everyone's busy and schedules are packed. Often, it's the things of God that get pushed to the margins.

But here's what I've learned: you'll always make time for what you value.

Being planted requires reprioritizing. It means choosing to build your life *around* God's House, not trying to squeeze it in when it's convenient. When you make church a non-negotiable, you begin to see the fruit that consistency brings.

2. Disappointment

Maybe you've been hurt by people in church. Maybe a leader let you down or someone gossiped or you felt overlooked. Now, there's a hesitation for you to re-engage.

Church hurt is real, but healing is real, too.

Every church has flaws. Every pastor is human. Don't let the imperfections of people keep you from the presence of God. Despite its imperfections, the church has still been the most influential force in my life. I've seen its beauty and its brokenness and I still believe in it.

If you've been wounded, give the church another chance. Ask God for the courage to trust again. Healing often begins when we take the step to replant our lives in community.

Sometimes it's not just the people, but it's the

pastors or leaders. You had expectations. You believed in someone and something happened that left you disillusioned.

Submission to spiritual authority isn't about perfect leaders. We have a perfect God who uses imperfect people.

Yes, be wise. Yes, discern character. However, don't allow disappointment to isolate you. Don't let one painful experience rob you of the covering and care that God intends to bring through leadership.

We'll talk more about spiritual covering in Chapter 6.

3. Fear of Commitment

In our culture, commitment can feel like a trap. What if something better comes along? What if I get bored? What if I mess up?

Spiritually speaking, commitment isn't restrictive. It's liberating and gives you direction, identity and purpose. When you say, *This is my church. These are my people. I'm here to grow, serve and build*, something shifts inside you. You are part of something bigger that will help to grow your life.

"Now you are the body of Christ, and each one of you is a part of it" (1 Corinthians 12:27).

Flourishing Comes With Time

In our "next big thing" culture, it's tempting to jump ship when things feel stale. But God often does His deepest work through faithful repetition, not instant results.

"To everything there is a season..." (Ecclesiastes 3:1 NKJV).

"Let perseverance finish its work so that you may be mature and complete, not lacking anything" (James 1:4).

It's the week-in/week-out rhythm of praise and worship, the accumulation of notes from God's Word, the small but consistent acts of serving others and years of building relationships that lead to long-term fruit.

Your Church Is Your Spiritual Home

Let me encourage you to stop waiting for the perfect moment to go all in. Stop church shopping. Stop treating church like a subscription that's easy to cancel when it doesn't meet your expectations.

Instead, ask God, *Where have You called me to be planted?*

When you find that place, treat it like your home. Show up early. Stay late. Invite others. Serve. Give. Pray for your pastors. Build relationships. Own the atmosphere. Be part of the solution. This is how you grow.

"...planted in the house of the Lord, they will flourish in the courts of our God" (Psalm 92:13).

Action Steps

Here are a few ways you can start (or restart) your journey of being planted in God's House:

- **Prioritize Sunday worship services.** Intentionally choose your attitude and the "posture of your heart" before you go so that you're in a place to receive what God has for you. Identify any practical barriers that may be standing in the way of consistent attendance, as well as any resistance you may be experiencing in your attitude, mindsets or emotions.

- **Serve consistently** on a team that fits with your gifts and passion.

- **Build meaningful relationships** in church. Join a small group, invite someone to coffee, open your life to knowing others and being known.

- **Give financially** to be a contributor, not just a consumer.

Reflection Questions

1. What thoughts and mindsets may have shifted in you around the idea of "being planted" in God's House after reading up to this point? Is there any place God is tugging at your heart?

2. Which, if any, of the barriers to being planted resonated with you? What shifts might you need to make in order to be planted in God's House in the way that the Bible talks about?

3. What's one area of your church life where you can "plant" more intentionally (time, serving, giving or relationships)?

FLOURISHING IN GOD'S HOUSE

FLOURISHING IN GOD'S HOUSE

"Blessed are those who dwell in your house..." (Psalm 84:4).

In Chapter 2, we talked about the importance of being planted and about staying rooted in a local church, committed and consistent. In this chapter, we're going to take that one step further and talk about what happens as a result of being planted: flourishing.

Let's go back to a theme passage in this book:

"The righteous will ***flourish*** *like a palm tree, they will grow like a cedar of Lebanon; planted in the house of the Lord, they will* ***flourish*** *in the courts of our God"* (Psalm 92:12–13).

In Hebrew, the word translated as flourish is "pārah." The root meaning is *to sprout, bud, blossom, bloom, break forth or fly up.*

It describes something coming to life, bursting open or thriving visibly—like a flower unfolding or a tree bursting into leaf after winter.

So when Psalm 92 says the righteous will *flourish*, it means they will come to life, grow and blossom abundantly in the presence of God. It's an image of vital growth, renewal and fruitfulness, not just survival.

Palm Trees: A Symbol of Vitality

In the ancient Near East, and especially in Hebrew culture, the date palm was one of the most honored and useful trees.

When Hebrew listeners would hear *"the righteous will flourish like a palm tree,"* they instantly pictured something deeply meaningful:

- **Palms were resilient:** They grew tall and strong in harsh, desert climates—bending but not breaking under intense wind or drought.
- **They were fruitful:** Each tree could yield hundreds of pounds of dates annually—a staple food and symbol of abundance.
- **They were evergreen:** Even when surrounding plants withered, palms stayed lush.
- **They were upright:** Their tall, straight trunks symbolized integrity and steadfastness.

So in Hebrew imagination, *to flourish like a palm tree* meant to stand firm through adversity, bear fruit over a lifetime and remain green and life-giving in every season.

Cedars of Lebanon: Stability and Legacy

The "cedar of Lebanon" was another vivid image.

These trees were:

- **Majestic and long-lived**—some lived over a thousand years.
- **Deep-rooted**—their roots spread wide, anchoring them through storms.
- **Valued**—Solomon used cedar wood to build the Temple (1 Kings 5–6).

Flourishing wasn't quick growth—it was enduring fruitfulness that came from *being deeply rooted in the right soil.* So when Psalm 92 says the righteous *"flourish in the courts of our God,"* it's about thriving because of proximity to divine life, not outward success.

We often think of flourishing as success or favor, but Biblical flourishing goes deeper. To flourish means to thrive in the fullness of God's purpose. It means you're growing spiritually, staying fresh emotionally, producing fruit relationally and living with vision generationally.

I want to highlight two things we see from this verse:

1. **Flourishing is possible.** In fact, it's not just

possible; it's God's plan for all believers. It's not just for "super Christians." The ability to flourish has been made available to all of us!

2. **Flourishing is a result of planting.** Even though God's design is for us all to flourish, it doesn't just happen. It's tied to where you're planted. You can't flourish in isolation. You flourish as *you're planted in the house of the Lord.*

John 15:5 tells us, "*He who abides in Me, and I in him, bears much fruit...*" (NKJV). This is what your life becomes when you stay rooted in God's House—strong, upright, lasting.

When we abide, when we stay connected to Him and stay planted in the soil He's called us to, we bear fruit. Trees don't grow overnight; they flourish over time. And so will you.

The Right Soil Matters

Let's go back to a picture we've seen before: the seed and the soil.

A seed has potential, but potential alone doesn't produce fruit. It needs **the right soil**. Soil that's rich with nutrients. Soil that's cared for. Soil that holds it steady through the storms.

"That person is like a tree planted by streams of water, which yields its fruit in season and whose leaf does not wither..." (Psalm 1:3).

The church is that kind of soil. It's the spiritual environment where your gifts, character and faith grow over time. You hear God's Word. You build relationships. You serve others. You learn to love and forgive. You discover your calling.

It's not always easy, but it's healthy. And healthy things grow.

You may be asking, *If I'm planted, why don't I feel like I'm flourishing yet?* And the answer usually is to just give it time. Roots grow before fruit shows.

Before you see it, God is strengthening it. Before it's public, God is making it personal. Before it's big, God is making it deep.

Growth That Includes Pruning

One part of flourishing that most people avoid is pruning. Flourishing isn't always comfortable. Sometimes it means God is cutting things back in your life. Not because He's disappointed or angry at you, but because He's growing you.

Jesus said:
"...every branch that does bear fruit he prunes so that it will be even more fruitful" (John 15:2).

Maybe you're in a season of pruning right now. Maybe God is removing distractions, attitudes or relationships. Maybe you're going through something painful, and you're wondering if you're doing something wrong.

But what if you're not doing anything wrong? What if you're just in the middle of your growth? What if this is the part where your roots go deeper?

Flourishing doesn't mean everything's easy. It means everything's fruitful. Even the hard seasons are producing something eternal.

Flourishing in Every Season

What does it look like to flourish in every season?

1. Trust and Deep Relationships Form

When you stay planted, you build long-term friendships. You stop restarting every six months. You get past surface-level and into real, honest and life-giving relationships.

This doesn't happen overnight. It takes time. But the reward is people who walk with you through victories and valleys.

"Two are better than one... If either of them falls down, one can help the other up" (Ecclesiastes 4:9–10).

2. Spiritual Maturity Develops

Planted believers stop living by feelings and start living by faith. They grow deeper in the Word. They develop a prayer life. They bear spiritual fruit (love, joy, peace, patience, etc.).

Believers who are growing and mature in their faith got there by staying planted.

3. Influence and Leadership Increase

God entrusts more to those who are faithful with what they have. When you serve with consistency, when you give generously, when you love people and build the church, you don't just grow. You begin to lead. Your voice matters. Your example matters. People watch how you live.

When you live planted, you give others a path to follow. That's how legacy is formed.

Flourishing Is Generational

When you get planted and stay planted, your life becomes a blessing to the generations that come after you.

We see this throughout Scripture:

"These commandments that I give you today are to be on your hearts. Impress them on your children. Talk about them when you sit at home and when you walk along the road..." (Deuteronomy 6:6–7).

"The promise is for you and your children..." (Acts 2:39).

"A good man leaves an inheritance to his children's children..." (Proverbs 13:22 NKJV).

When a family is planted in God's House, their children grow up in the presence of God. They serve alongside their parents. They see faith modeled. They find their own sense of belonging.

I've seen many families who planted themselves in a local church and never looked back. Decades later, their kids are leading worship, their grandkids are in the youth group and their family name is known as one that helped build the House.

That's legacy. That's what it means to flourish across generations.

Flourishing Often Feels Ordinary

Flourishing is about quiet, steady growth that lasts. Most of the time, flourishing looks pretty ordinary:

- Showing up week after week.
- Serving without applause.
- Giving faithfully in every season.
- Leading a small group even when you're busy.
- Forgiving when it's hard.
- Worshiping when you don't feel like it.

This is the slow, unseen work that leads to spiritual depth. But just because it's unseen doesn't mean it's insignificant. The prophet Isaiah said, *"...take root downward, And bear fruit upward"*
(Isaiah 37:31 NKJV).

Roots grow first. Fruit comes later. We want the results, but God wants the roots. Ultimately, the roots aren't as glamorous and visible as the branches of a tree, but they are what hold it steady in a storm. And the same is true for us.

The Bamboo Principle

There's a story often told about the Chinese bamboo tree. After it's planted, you water and fertilize it daily, but for the first four years, you see almost nothing above the surface. Then in the fifth year, it suddenly starts growing. It can grow up to 90 feet tall in just six weeks.

Did it grow in six weeks? No, it grew in five years. You just couldn't see it.

That's what flourishing looks like in the kingdom of God. Sometimes you feel like you're doing all the right things but not seeing the results.

Don't stop.

Keep watering. Keep showing up. Keep serving. Because when your breakthrough comes, it will be because you stayed planted.

"Let us not become weary in doing good, for at the proper time we will reap a harvest..." (Galatians 6:9).

Flourish Where You're Planted

If you want to flourish, you need to fully engage with the church God has called you to.

That means letting go of the "what if" questions: *What if there's a better opportunity? What if this church isn't as exciting as the one across town? What if I get bored?*

These questions don't lead to growth—they lead to perpetual wandering. Our culture has saturated us with options, and it can make us obsessed with finding the best option and what suits our desires and convenience best at that moment. However, this mentality runs contrary to how God operates and how He brings blessing into our lives.

God has graced you for a place.

"But now God has placed the members, each one of them, in the body, just as He desired."
(1 Corinthians 12:18 NASB).

You're not there by accident. He placed you there on purpose, for a purpose. When you get planted where God placed you, you stop looking for greener grass and start watering your own. Instead...

You build.
You serve.
You lead.

You give.

You stay.

Many people never flourish because they stay in a consumer mindset. They approach church like a product for their benefit and enjoyment, entertainment or convenience: *Was the message good today? Did I like the worship? Was the parking a hassle?*

But a contributor shows up differently: *Who can I encourage today? Where can I serve? What's God doing in the life of this church, and how can I be part of it?*

This is such a pivotal shift, and even though it may seem counterintuitive, I've talked with many people whose church experience completely changed and their life began to truly flourish when they made this shift in their mentality.

"It is more blessed to give than to receive" (Acts 20:35).

"...whoever refreshes others will be refreshed" (Proverbs 11:25).

You don't grow by spectating.

You grow by *participating.*

You don't flourish by consuming.

You flourish by *contributing.*

Build Your Life Today With Your Future in Mind

What kind of legacy do you want to leave? What kind of example are you setting for your children or the people watching your life?

Flourishing in God's House is not just about your personal growth. It's about:

- The future marriages you'll impact.
- The leaders you'll raise up.
- The students you'll disciple.
- The friends who will come to faith because you stayed faithful.

"This is to my Father's glory, that you bear much fruit, showing yourselves to be my disciples" (John 15:8).

"Unless the Lord builds the house, the builders labor in vain..." (Psalm 127:1).

God is building something and when you join Him, your life becomes part of something eternal.

Action Steps

Here's how you can start flourishing right where you are:

- **Take an inventory of how you spend your time, effort and energy and do an audit on your priorities.** What do you spend your time on each day, each week, each month, each year? Do your schedule and energy output match your values and priorities?

- **Write a list of your top priorities that you want to define your life.** Consider whether the life you're living now will lead you to the legacy you want to leave. If not, identify and write down what adjustments you need to make for that to be true. If your top priorities do reflect the life you want to live and the legacy you want to leave, what will you do to make sure you stay committed to these priorities and don't drift? (Share with an accountability partner or mentor, plan a yearly review with your spouse, etc.)

- **Choose to stay faithful through every season.** Don't uproot in the hard seasons and don't drift in the easy seasons. Faithfulness is a choice and requires intentionality. It isn't easy, but it is something God rewards, and it is worth it—even if we don't see the results immediately.

Reflection Questions

1. What does "flourishing" look like in your life right now and what would it take to grow in this season?

2. Have you ever been tempted to "uproot" yourself when things got hard? What helped you stay? Is there a place you're feeling challenged in this area right now? What action step can you take to support your commitment to staying faithful to what God has called you to?

3. Is there anyone in your life who has modeled long-term faithfulness in the church? What have you learned from them?

4. Think about the life you are building and the legacy you are creating. What are you building your life around? Will it last for eternity, or are you devoting your life to things that lose meaning? What will your kids or friends say about your commitment to God's House?

BETTER TOGETHER

BETTER TOGETHER

When you give your life to Jesus, you're not just saved from sin; you're brought into a family. The Bible describes our faith journey in relational terms: sons and daughters, brothers and sisters, the household of God.

God is a Father. When you give your life to Him, you're adopted into His family.

"But to all who believed him and accepted him, he gave the right to become children of God" (John 1:12 NLT).

"Instead, you received God's Spirit when he adopted you as his own children. Now we call him, 'Abba, Father'" (Romans 8:15 NLT).

"God decided in advance to adopt us into his own family by bringing us to himself through Jesus Christ. This is what he wanted to do, and it gave him great pleasure" (Ephesians 1:5 NLT).

The local church is where that family connection becomes visible and transformational.

The Church Isn't Just a Crowd. It's a Family.

One phrase I have heard churches use (including ours)

is "Welcome Home." I like the way it sounds and what it represents. We want every person to feel like they're not just walking into a crowd of people. They are walking into a place where they belong—a home, a **spiritual home.** We want them to build their life here. To get past the "hello" stage. To move from visitor to family. To stop wondering if they fit and start realizing they're needed.

When you begin to see the church as a family to belong to, everything changes. Sunday isn't an event. Small groups aren't optional. Serving isn't a favor. It's all a part of family life. You begin to realize that you're not just here for yourself. You are here for what we're building together.

And the best part? You don't have to earn your place or prove you belong.

A spiritual family doesn't wait for perfect conditions. It opens the door. It sets the table. It builds a place where people can grow, heal, serve and lead.

"Consequently, you are no longer foreigners and strangers, but fellow citizens with God's people and also members of his household" (Ephesians 2:19).

God's House isn't just where you go. It's where you belong.

God Sets the Lonely in Families

So many people today are battling loneliness. It's an epidemic. We have more digital connections than ever, and yet people are more isolated, more anxious and more relationally fragmented than ever before.

The Bible gives us God's solution: *"God sets the lonely in families..."* (Psalm 68:6).

God's design to heal loneliness and isolation is not just individual comfort. It's a relational connection. Notice the verse doesn't say that the lonely are set in friendships. God sets us in families.

The local church is a spiritual family. When you step into the environment of a healthy local church, powerful, supernatural things begin to happen. The environment of a strong local church can help heal your heart through relationships.

Spiritual Healing Happens in Relationships

You may have heard the phrase "hurt people hurt people," but there's also a flip side. "Healed people heal people."

When you're planted in the House of God, you begin to experience something deeply restorative. Not just from the worship or teaching, but from the people.

Conversations after service, encouragement from someone in your small group, a text when you're struggling, a prayer in the lobby. This kind of connection can't happen if you stay distant. You have to let people in.

You'll never experience the full power of God's House until you allow yourself to be **seen, known and loved.**

"If one part suffers, every part suffers with it; if one part is honored, every part rejoices with it"
(1 Corinthians 12:26).

That's what family does. It shares the weight. It celebrates the win. It stands with you in every season. It's also where transformation happens.

You Can't Grow Alone

Spiritual growth is deeply relational. Read and study your Bible, have personal prayer time, listen to God-inspired podcasts. These are all good things, but they can't replace *people*. God uses people to grow us.

"As iron sharpens iron, so one person sharpens another" (Proverbs 27:17).

There's no such thing as a solo Christian. A Christian without a church is a contradiction in terms. In the early church, believers listened to teaching while they lived in community.

"They devoted themselves to the apostles' teaching and to fellowship, to the breaking of bread and to prayer...They broke bread in their homes and ate together with glad and sincere hearts"
(Acts 2:42, 46).

This wasn't optional. It wasn't occasional. It was the normal rhythm of life in God's family. And the result? Growth. Strength. Fruitfulness. Joy. It's still true today.

Relationships That Help You Grow

Not every relationship in the church is automatically life-giving. Like any family, there are people with different personalities, ideas and maturity levels. When you press in, when you're vulnerable and when you choose connection over comfort, you begin to find your people. These are the relationships that call out the best in us. We all need people who can sharpen us, pray for us and challenge us. We need people who speak truth in love and walk with us through the valleys. These relationships won't just happen. You have to be intentional.

Be the kind of friend you want to have. Go to the event. Start the conversation. Show up when it's inconvenient. Stay when it's uncomfortable.

Over time, you'll realize something powerful: **you're not alone anymore.**

If the enemy can't keep you from salvation, he'll try to keep you from life-giving community. He'll use offense. He'll use comparison. He'll use pride. Without you recognizing it, isolation starts to feel normal. Scripture is very clear. Isolation is dangerous.

"A man who isolates himself seeks his own desire; He rages against all wise judgment" (Proverbs 18:1 NKJV).

Isolation leads to deception. You start thinking you don't need anyone and that you're better off alone. That church is optional. But that's a lie. You weren't designed to grow in solitude. You were designed to grow in relationship with other people.

You Need a Church and a Pastor

A Christian without a church is not living in alignment with God's design. Yes, your salvation is personal. But your growth is relational. **You need a spiritual family, and you need spiritual leaders.**

In the New Testament, believers were always connected to a church, led by spiritual leaders and cared for in community.

"...not giving up meeting together, as some are in the habit of doing, but encouraging one another..." (Hebrews 10:25).

"...each member belongs to all the others" (Romans 12:5).

The church is people, gathered and growing together under spiritual covering. We'll talk more about covering in the next chapter, but you must realize that your pastor can't help you if you're not connected. You can't be led if you're not known. You can't be encouraged if you're not present.

Don't Quit When It Gets Hard

It's so important to understand: relationships in the church are not built on perfection. They're built on commitment. Spiritual family sounds great, until people disappoint you.

Just like in a natural family, there will be conflict, misunderstandings and offenses. When you choose to stay planted, even through friction, something powerful happens. You grow.

"Be completely humble and gentle; be patient, bearing with one another in love" (Ephesians 4:2).

Knowing how to forgive is a sign of spiritual maturity. It's choosing unity over division. Grace over judgment. Restoration over cancellation.

Making the Church Your Home

If you're going to flourish relationally, you have to treat the local church like home.

Home means permanent. It means showing up, even when you're tired. It means serving, even when it costs you. It means staying, even when someone hurts your feelings. You don't walk away from your church because of one rough conversation. You lean in. You grow up. You work it out.

Here's what happens when you do:

- Trust deepens.
- Relationships mature.
- Influence grows.
- Your life becomes a picture of God's grace.

And maybe most importantly, your church becomes a place where others can feel safe to do the same.

Be the One

So many people are waiting for their church to be what they hope for. But what if you stopped waiting and started becoming?

Be the one who invites. Be the one who checks in. Be the one who stays long enough to help build what others only dream about.

"Each of you should use whatever gift you have received to serve others..." (1 Peter 4:10).

"Carry each other's burdens..." (Galatians 6:2).

You don't need to have it all together. You just need to show up with a heart that says, *This is my church. These are my people. I'm not going anywhere.*

Action Steps

Here are a few ways you can build deeper spiritual relationships and make your church a true home:

- **Find a place to make a commitment—one that allows you to know others and be known by them**. Joining a small group, serving on a team or finding another way to consistently connect with God's House and other believers can have a powerful impact on your life. It's one of the best ways to move from being a spectator to pursuing and building real relationships. This is also one of the ways where we experience some of the richest and deepest blessings of the "flourishing" that God designed us to experience through being planted in His House.

- **Be an initiator.** Don't always be the one who is waiting to be invited. Some of the greatest rewards in life require initiative, risk and vulnerability! It may take you outside your comfort zone, but that's okay. It's how we grow! Make a new friend. Ask someone to coffee. Get to know someone after service. Don't just show up as service starts and run out when it's done. Intentionally create margin for relational growth in your life.

- **Show up consistently.** Relationships don't grow without time. Prioritize Sunday worship and stay long enough to be known.

- **Stay through the friction.** Relationships—even good, healthy ones—will inevitably have times when they feel uncomfortable, or even painful. When conflict or offense comes, choose to lean in and not walk out. Remember, the Bible tells us that iron sharpens iron. This is how God works in us to refine us and help make us more like Him. When we stay through the friction, not only do we grow, we position ourselves to receive the blessing that is on the other side.

Reflection Questions

1. What do you think it means to belong to a spiritual family, not just attend a church?

2. Are you truly known by anyone in your church? If not, consider why not and what might be the reason for that. What step can you take to build deeper relationships?

3. What would change in your faith if you fully embraced your church as family? Not just a place to go, but a home to build?

THE LOCAL CHURCH —YOUR SPIRITUAL COVERING

THE LOCAL CHURCH—YOUR SPIRITUAL COVERING

We all need a place where our souls can rest, be guided and grow strong. Life can be unpredictable—seasons of hardship, spiritual attack and weariness will come. In His kindness, God designed a place of safety and strength for His people: the local church. It's where we find spiritual family, godly leadership and the covering we need to stay steady through every storm.

When it rains, you look for an umbrella. That's what spiritual covering is—protection. Just as an umbrella shields you from the elements, spiritual covering protects you from exposure to things that would otherwise leave you vulnerable. One of the clearest ways God provides that covering is through the local church.

In a world that celebrates independence, autonomy and self-made strength, the idea of spiritual covering can feel countercultural. But throughout the entire Bible, we see that God's pattern has always involved divine order, spiritual authority and community. He uses leaders to guide His people, establishes structures that sustain them, and blesses those who choose to come under His design. The local church isn't just a place where you grow. It's a place where you're covered.

God's Design for Covering

The apostle Paul is widely recognized as one of the earliest and most influential church planters in Christian history. In 1 Corinthians 14:33, as he's teaching the church in Corinth how to lead and pastor the people, he talks about how God is not a God of disorder. He doesn't work in chaos or confusion. Instead, Paul says He is the God of peace.

The word for *peace* used here in the original language is "eirenē", meaning to *join, tie together into a whole.* It paints the picture of peace being "God's gift of wholeness" that comes when all essential parts are joined together the right way. God's design for our lives is always for a reason and will always position us for what is best.

If we want the peace of wholeness, we have to look at what God has designed and how we fit into those things.

God has established three primary institutions on earth to bring order and protection into our lives: the family, the government and the church. Each one is designed to provide a unique kind of covering:

- Family brings relational and emotional covering.
- Government brings legal and civil covering.
- The church brings spiritual covering.

"Let everyone be subject to the governing authorities, for there is no authority except that which God has established" (Romans 13:1).

Though this verse refers to government, the principle applies broadly: authority originates from God. When we align ourselves under that authority, we position ourselves under His blessing and protection.

In the church, this covering is expressed through *spiritual leadership:* pastors and leaders who are called to guide, equip and care for God's people.

The Role of a Pastor

The image of a shepherd caring for his flock runs throughout Scripture, and in the New Testament, this picture becomes the defining model for pastoral ministry. The very word *pastor* comes from the Latin "pastor", meaning *shepherd.* In Greek, the word "poimēn" is used to describe both literal shepherds and spiritual leaders.

Jesus called Himself the Good Shepherd (John 10:11), the one who lays down His life for His sheep. Paul lists "pastors and teachers" among the gifts Christ gives the church—literally, "shepherds and teachers" (Ephesians 4:11). Peter echoes this in 1 Peter 5:2–4, urging church leaders:

"Be shepherds of God's flock that is under your care, watching over them—not because you must, but because you are willing...not lording it over those entrusted to you, but being examples to the flock. And when the Chief Shepherd appears, you will receive the crown of glory that will never fade away."

Christ is the Chief Shepherd, and local pastors are under-shepherds called to lead, feed, guide and protect those entrusted to their care. Their leadership is not domineering, but nurturing. Not self-serving, but sacrificial. Not controlling, but caring.

Believers flourish under the spiritual covering of godly leadership. A pastor's role is to create a safe, spiritually rich environment where people can mature in faith, remain connected to the body and be equipped to live out their God-given calling.

When we connect this truth to Psalm 92:13—that those who are planted in the house of the Lord, will flourish in the courts of our God—we see that flourishing happens not in isolation and independence, but under care and community. Believers thrive when they are planted in the living rhythm of a local church, with Christ as the head of the church and local pastors serving and leading to care for the "flock" or the members of the church they've been entrusted with.

"God has put all things under the authority of Christ and has made him head over all things for the benefit of the church" (Ephesians 1:22 NLT).

Colossians 1 in The Message version paints a beautiful picture of Christ as the head of the church and God's heart for the order and authority He's designed. We'll look more at what the overflow of living in alignment with that authority does in our lives, but for right now, let me just draw your attention to what it says about God's divine structure, authority and Christ as the head of the church:

"...We look at this Son and see God's original purpose in everything created. For everything, absolutely everything, above and below, visible and invisible, rank after rank after rank of angels—everything got started in him and finds its purpose in him. He was there before any of it came into existence and holds it all together right up to this moment. And when it comes to the church, he organizes and holds it together, like a head does a body." (Colossians 1:15–18 MSG).

What God Intended for Spiritual Authority

For some, the word authority may bring up a lot of

negative feelings or pain. Maybe you've experienced leadership that wounded instead of healed, or maybe you've seen control disguised as care. You may have suffered spiritual abuse or seen leadership used to manipulate. Sadly, there are moments when human leaders have allowed their ego to go unchecked and misused their position of authority for personal gain, bringing harm and pain rather than healing and protection to others. That is wrong. That is *never* God's heart.

In fact, the Bible is clear that leaders should steward their character and influence with great care:

James 3:1 warns, *"Not many of you should become teachers, my brothers, for you know that we who teach will be judged with greater strictness"* (ESV).

We also see an incredibly strong admonition from Jesus to His disciples in Matthew 18:6:

"But whoever causes one of these little ones who believe in and acknowledge and cleave to Me to stumble and sin [that is, who entices him or hinders him in right conduct or thought], it would be better (more expedient and profitable or advantageous) for him to have a great millstone fastened around his neck and to be sunk in the depth of the sea" (AMPC).

What we see here is that God hates abuse and takes it seriously when someone misuses their power and authority. Jesus is teaching His disciples about humility, responsibility and the seriousness of spiritual influence. "Little ones" refers both to children and to humble believers who have placed their trust in Him. The point is clear: spiritual leaders or those with influence carry great responsibility not to harm or mislead those who are young or vulnerable in faith.

True authority in God's design always protects, empowers and restores.

God never calls leaders to dominate; He calls them to serve. Jesus made that clear when He said, *"...whoever wants to become great among you must be your servant"* (Matthew 20:26).

Spiritual covering is about alignment. It's choosing to live under God's design, trusting the shepherds He's placed in our lives to help guide and guard us. Healthy leaders don't remove your ability to hear from God; they help you discern His voice more clearly.

That's why the Bible speaks so directly to both sides of the relationship between shepherds and their flock: *"Be shepherds of God's flock that is under your care, watching over them—not because you must, but because you are willing... not lording it over those entrusted to you, but being examples to the flock"* (1 Peter 5:2-3).

And to the flock:

"Have confidence in your leaders and submit to their authority, because they keep watch over you as those who must give an account" (Hebrews 13:17).

This kind of relationship is built on trust and mutual honor, not control. God designed spiritual authority as a flow of protection and blessing. The shepherd guides, feeds and guards the flock; the sheep listen, follow and stay close to receive the benefits of that care.

Of course, your ultimate covering is always Christ Himself, the Chief Shepherd. Pastors and leaders are simply His under-shepherds, appointed to help you grow in faith and flourish in the community of believers. Living under godly leadership doesn't limit freedom. It brings strength and safety.

When this relationship works as God intended, something powerful happens. Trust thrives, healing happens, faith deepens and unity grows. The church becomes a living expression of God's care: a covering that protects, provides and guides into growth. Not a place of control, but of flourishing.

Everyone Follows Someone

Every flock needs a shepherd. Every believer needs spiritual leadership.

Growth never happens in isolation—athletes have coaches, students have teachers, soldiers have commanders, business leaders have mentors. Every environment of growth involves guidance. Your spiritual life is no different.

Just as sheep depend on the shepherd's voice for guidance and protection, we depend on spiritual leaders who help us discern God's direction and stay grounded in truth.

We live in a world that celebrates self-sufficiency and "DIY spirituality." Many believers today have teachers they listen to, podcasts they follow and authors they quote, but no one who truly *knows* them. There's nothing wrong with learning from gifted voices, but it's not the same as being pastored in the context of a local body of believers.

A pastor doesn't just teach from a distance; they walk with you up close. They know your story, your strengths and your struggles. They're present in the valleys and on the mountaintops. A podcast can inspire you, but your pastor can *cover* you.

Inspiration can happen from a distance; impartation happens through relationship.

A pastor is someone you can look in the eye. Someone who knows your name, prays for you and helps you walk out your faith in community. This kind of relationship turns information into transformation and it moves you from being inspired to being formed. Don't settle for distant inspiration when God wants to give you the irreplaceable richness of relational impartation. It's worth it and it's part of God's design.

You may find yourself in a larger church where it's harder to have a close, personal relationship with the lead pastor. And that's okay. That doesn't mean you're uncovered or unseen.

In a healthy church, spiritual covering is shared and multiplied through layers of trusted leaders—pastors, team leaders, small group leaders, coaches and mentors. While the lead pastor may provide overall spiritual authority and vision, you should have someone in your church who knows you personally and is helping you grow spiritually.

If you're not personally connected to your lead pastor, find someone in the church who carries spiritual authority. Someone trusted, available and spiritually mature. This might be a campus pastor, a small group leader, a ministry leader or the person who leads the team you serve on. Ask questions, build a relationship, invite their leadership into your life and let them speak into your growth.

Spiritual covering is ultimately about alignment with spiritual leadership. In a large church, relational access to the lead pastor isn't always possible, but that doesn't mean you're spiritually disconnected. What matters most is that you are known, cared for and aligned with the heart and direction of God's House and living under healthy accountability and spiritual guidance.

I probably don't need to state the obvious, but your pastor needs to be a real person! You might be laughing, but in the age of AI, that needs to be said! And your pastor needs to be at the same church where you are planted. Again, don't make the mistake of thinking you can receive all the benefits of a pastor and a local church through a YouTube Channel or by someone who is living in another city. I'm not saying those things don't add something to your life, but it's different than a local church and a local church pastor.

"For though you have countless guides in Christ, you do not have many fathers. For I became your father in Christ Jesus through the gospel"
1 Corinthians 4:15 (ESV).

Paul the Apostle is addressing this issue in 1 Corinthians. On this Christian journey, there will be so many people who will add to our lives with guidance and teaching and encouragement, but there will only be a few who will be like spiritual fathers and provide a spiritual covering in our lives.

I've had so many mentors in my life who have made some amazing spiritual deposits. However, I've only ever had two pastors. Those relationships were life-changing and shaped me and the trajectory of my life. This is a key that many people miss out on because they don't realize the importance of pressing in and having a pastor, a spiritual father, in their lives.

The Power and Blessing of Unity

Unity invites the blessing of God and it comes through order and alignment. When a church is led well, there will be unity and strength. The result will be God's blessing. You can feel it in the atmosphere. There's peace. Clarity. Anointing. God's hand rests on that House.

"How good and pleasant it is when God's people live together in unity...For there the Lord bestows His blessing..." (Psalm 133:1, 3).

One of the only recorded prayers that Jesus prayed for you and me involved unity.

"My prayer is not for them alone. I pray also for those who will believe in me through their message, that all of them may be one, Father, just as you are in me and I am in you. May they also be in us so that the world may believe that you have sent me. I have given them the glory that you gave me, that they may be one as we are one—I in them and you in me—so that they may be brought to complete unity. Then the world will know that you sent me and have loved them even as you have loved me" (John 17:20–23).

Think about how important this must be to Jesus.

And how His heart must break when there is division in the church.

When there is division and disorder in any environment, there will be strife. Confusion. Drift. When things are in misalignment, they don't work right. If the wheels on a car are out of alignment, the vehicle pulls to one side, the tires wear unevenly and the ride is bumpy and inefficient—everything suffers until the alignment is corrected. The same is true in the church.

This is why unity is important, healthy spiritual leadership is so vital and it matters that you're in a healthy church that values godly unity. Unity doesn't mean uniformity. We don't have to all be the same.

The key is that we are all seeking to live God's way and to honor Him with our lives and reflect His image in our lives and in our world. When you're under the umbrella of a healthy house that is unified, there is blessing and supernatural protection.

What Are a Pastor's Responsibilities?

Let's talk about what spiritual leadership and being a pastor looks like practically. The work of a shepherd involves:

1. Feeding—Preaching and teaching the Word of God. A shepherd's first calling is to nourish the flock with truth.

"Feed my sheep" (John 21:17).

"Preach the word; be prepared in season and out of season; correct, rebuke and encourage—with great patience and careful instruction" (2 Timothy 4:2).

A faithful pastor ensures that the people under their care grow strong in Scripture and are equipped to live it out daily.

2. Guiding—Providing vision and leadership to the church. A good shepherd gives direction that aligns with God's heart and Word.

"Where there is no vision, the people perish..." (Proverbs 29:18 KJV).

"Then I will give you shepherds after my own heart, who will lead you with knowledge and understanding" (Jeremiah 3:15).

Pastors are called to guide God's people toward His purposes. Helping them find their place in His story and walk faithfully in it.

3. Protecting—Warning against false teaching and ungodly cultural practices. Shepherds protect the flock from spiritual danger.

"Keep watch over yourselves and all the flock of which the Holy Spirit has made you overseers. Be shepherds of the church of God, which he bought with his own blood" (Acts 20:28).

"Dear friends, do not believe every spirit, but test the spirits to see whether they are from God, because many false prophets have gone out into the world" (1 John 4:1).

A loving leader guards their people not through fear or control but through discernment, truth and courage.

4. Caring—Walking with people through transition, pain and difficulty. A true shepherd doesn't abandon the flock when life gets hard.

"Carry each other's burdens, and in this way you will fulfill the law of Christ" (Galatians 6:2).

"He tends his flock like a shepherd: He gathers the lambs in his arms and carries them close to his heart..." (Isaiah 40:11).

A pastor's heart reflects the compassion of Jesus, the Good Shepherd who stays close to the hurting and walks with His people through the valleys.

When we have carefully chosen a church with godly leadership, we can trust those leaders to safely guide us to do the job God has given us to do. That's the heart of Hebrews 13:17:

"Have confidence in your leaders and submit to their authority, because they keep watch over you as those who must give an account."

Pastors will answer to God for how they lead. You have a part to play by using wisdom and discernment to choose a local church to plant yourself that's led by a leader committed to integrity. Then choose to honor their God-given authority and leadership, follow with humility and allow those in spiritual leadership to disciple you in your faith.

How to Receive From Your Pastor

It's one thing to attend a church and it's another to truly plant your heart there, to open your life to the leadership from a surrendered place and to let God use your pastor to speak into your life. When you choose to receive from your pastor, you're saying, *I'm open. I want to grow.*

Here are a few ways to position your heart to receive and flourish under godly leadership:

- **Have a humble, expectant heart**. Each time you gather, come ready to hear from God. He often speaks through your pastor's words in ways you don't expect.
- **Lean in and take notes.** Writing down what stands out helps you reflect later and apply truth to your everyday life.
- **Put it into practice.** Growth happens when we don't just listen but we live it out. Ask, *How can I walk this out this week?*
- **Pray for your pastor.** Ministry is sacred work, and your prayers strengthen the one who's leading and caring for your church family.
- **Trust the process.** Growth often stretches us. When God uses your pastor's teaching to challenge or shape you, remember that it's all part of His refining work in your life.

Receiving from your pastor is about humility and partnership. It's saying, *God, I trust You enough to let someone You've called help guide me closer to You.*

Paul wrote, *"Follow my example, as I follow the example of Christ"* (1 Corinthians 11:1). That's the heart of spiritual leadership and the beauty of being covered. It's not so much about elevating a person as it is about following someone who is themselves following Jesus. When you choose to trust godly leadership, you're aligning your life with God's design for community, protection and growth. And it's within that covering—imperfect though human leaders may be—that we discover the safety, strength and stability our hearts long for.

The Power of Choosing to Live an Aligned Life

If spiritual covering is God's design, then the question becomes deeply personal: Who is covering you? Who are you submitted to? Who is speaking into your life and watching over your soul?

For many believers, the answer is uncertain. They may attend church, but have still not created a life that is surrendered and submitted to the spiritual authority of their local church.

A shepherd's role is not just to preach. It's to know, guide and guard the flock. There is safety in being known. There is strength in belonging. And there is peace in being aligned with the shepherds God has placed in your life.

Being under spiritual covering is a choice to live in alignment with God's order and trust His design for you to flourish. When you're planted under godly leadership, you don't give up your voice; you discover the vehicle designed to refine it and position it for its God-given purpose.

Alignment is not something God will force on us. But what I know to be true, from God's Word and my own life experience, is that choosing to live aligned is positioning yourself to live blessed. Not necessarily in a way where everything is easy and nothing goes wrong, but the kind of blessing that comes when we are where God has called us to be. This is a place of faith-filled surrender and trust, where authority and anointing flow freely, where faith takes root and where your life can bear lasting fruit.

Action Steps

Here's how you can start living under spiritual covering today:

- **Decide where you're planted and who your spiritual authority is**. Settle the question: In my church, who is the spiritual leader God has placed in my life right now?

- **Position yourself to receive.** Examine your heart and be intentional with both your attitude and actions. Show up with expectancy. Serve with humility. Apply what you hear in your daily life.

- **Cultivate a spirit of honor for God and the authority He's placed you under.** "Submitted to authority" doesn't mean "weak." We can be strong and humble at the same time. Have a soft heart and a teachable spirit. Nurture unity in your church. Speak life over your leaders. Be a source of encouragement and blessing to those who help build your faith.

Reflection Questions

1. How have you viewed spiritual leadership in your life up to this point? Do you feel like your life is submitted to godly authority in the way that God designed it to be?

2. What did you notice as you read this chapter? Did you experience any topics that convicted you, challenged you, comforted you or compelled you to make a change in your thoughts or actions? If so, continue to ask God to lead you and work on any areas of your heart that He may want to bring change or clarity to.

GOD'S UNFOLDING PURPOSE

GOD'S UNFOLDING PURPOSE

For many people, discovering their purpose feels like chasing something just out of reach. They're waiting for a sign, a divine whisper or a moment of revelation that will suddenly make everything clear.

More often than not, purpose doesn't arrive with fireworks and fanfare. It's a process that unfolds. And a significant part of our spiritual purpose unfolds best within the context of the local church.

You were created on purpose, with purpose, for a purpose. You weren't designed to discover your purpose alone. God's plan for your calling is directly connected to the people and the place He's assigned to your life. In the church, you can begin to recognize, refine and release the purpose God has placed inside of you.

You Were Made for This

Let's start with a truth that applies to every believer:

"For we are God's masterpiece. He has created us anew in Christ Jesus, so we can do the good things he planned for us long ago" (Ephesians 2:10 NLT).

God has already prepared good works for you. The

question is not *if* you have a purpose, but it's *where* and *how* you'll begin to walk it out.

I found my purpose in the local church. As I got involved in my church by serving, showing up and saying yes, I began to discover gifts I didn't know I had. I didn't realize I could lead. I didn't know I could communicate. I certainly didn't see myself pastoring one day. Being planted in God's House created an environment where those gifts were drawn out.

Discovering purpose isn't just for people called to ministry. God awakens purpose for anyone willing to open their heart and take simple steps of faith.

Purpose isn't a one-time discovery. It's an unfolding journey. Think of a folded piece of paper with layers inside. As you open each section, more is revealed. That's what it's like to walk in your God-given purpose and calling. You start with what's in front of you, and as you're faithful, God reveals more.

Where Does It Begin?

I believe serving is one of the most significant ways you can activate the gifts God has placed in your life. Partly because it forces you to stop looking inward and start living outward. Your faith begins to take shape. The truth is, serving can seem so simple and elementary and inconsequential. I think that's partly why God uses it. In a sense, it's a test.

"Each of you should use whatever gift you have received to serve others, as faithful stewards of God's grace in its various forms" (1 Peter 4:10).

We've all been given a gift, and the best way to see the gift developed is by putting it in God's hands and serving other people.

This is why we emphasize serving in our church. It's not because we need to fill volunteer slots, but because serving is where purpose comes alive.

I've seen it time and time again. Someone joins the parking team or the kids team or the worship team, not thinking much of it. In the process, something shifts. They find joy. Confidence. Community. Before long, they're walking in a rhythm that's bigger than themselves.

They didn't find their purpose by searching for it. They found it by serving their way into it.

Jesus modeled the significance of serving:

"For even the Son of Man did not come to be served, but to serve, and to give his life as a ransom for many" (Mark 10:45).

If Jesus served, we should serve. The church is the best place to walk out and grow in your faith. Through serving, we become more like Jesus.

"From him the whole body, joined and held together by every supporting ligament, grows and builds itself up in love, as each part does its work"
(Ephesians 4:16).

Your part matters. Your purpose contributes to the health of the whole body. Until you step into your role, something will be missing. Not just in you, but in the church.

The Toolbox Was Always There

Imagine you inherit a toolbox filled with equipment you've never used before. You know there's value in there, but it's unfamiliar. So you start building small things, practicing, learning. You slowly begin to realize: *These tools fit my hands. This is what I was made to build.*

That's what gifts are like. You already have them. God

put them inside of you, but often they don't make sense until you start using them. Sometimes, you may even discover a gift you didn't know you had through serving. By simply doing something to fill a gap, you discover a gift or passion. Or, sometimes a leader will see something in you that you didn't even see in yourself and help develop it in you. We may not always know the gifts and talents and abilities that God has given us. But He does, and as we're faithful, He'll help those things begin to unfold.

Faithfulness Helps Us Find and Refine Our Gifts and Calling

I could share countless stories of people who discovered or developed gifts through serving in God's House. One young woman began attending our church as a teenager. She got involved in youth and planted herself in our local church. She eventually started serving and continued to grow, giving her time, heart and energy to building His church.

Some of her friends served on the Capture Team (the team responsible for photography), so she decided to sign up for the team and join them. She had never taken pictures or really been involved in photography before, but as she served her leaders noticed she had a natural gift. Over the next couple of years, they taught her, coached her and helped her develop this talent she had discovered.

Her experience serving in the church gave her the confidence to take a step and start doing photography professionally. It's been amazing to see what has taken place over the years, going from a volunteer with no knowledge or experience in photography to a full-time business. She still serves on the Capture Team using that gift to serve and build God's House today.

What a beautiful example of how serving in church can bring out and develop a God-given gift. Photography wasn't on this young woman's radar as a gift or a passion she possessed, but it was something that she discovered and developed through serving in church. This is the beauty of serving and faithfulness. Through her willingness and faithfulness to serve and the faithfulness of the team leaders who developed her, there is a ripple effect of blessing. God's House is blessed by her gift, she and her family are blessed by the income her business provides and the clients she serves are blessed by her creativity and skill. That gift was always there. It just needed the right opportunity, environment and people to help it be discovered and developed. *Serving was the process that brought out what God deposited in her and had a plan for all along.*

It's Not About a Title

We tend to think of purpose in terms of roles like pastor, missionary or teacher. It's important to distinguish that those are assignments, not someone's identity.

Purpose is about discovering who God created you to be and what He created you to do in this world. Purpose is also about being faithful with what's in your hand. It's about doing what God has called you to do today and trusting Him to unfold what comes next.

Earlier, we talked about flourishing through faithfulness. This is what that looks like in action: serving week after week, leading when no one sees, encouraging someone in the hallway, showing up early to make coffee, staying late to reset a room after a service.

It won't feel glamorous, but it's purpose in motion. God sees it and He uses it.

Faithfulness Comes Before Fulfillment

There's a pattern in Scripture that's impossible to ignore: faithfulness is what lays the foundation for fulfillment.

- Joseph was faithful in Potiphar's house before ruling in Pharaoh's palace.
- David served his father's sheep before he led the nation of Israel.
- Ruth was faithful in the field of Boaz before becoming part of the royal line.
- Peter served as a disciple before becoming a pillar in the church.

None of these Bible characters rushed their calling. They stayed planted, served and submitted. Their purpose was unfolding in the process of being faithful day in and day out.

The same is true for you. You don't need to chase your purpose. You just need to steward your current season. When you show God you're faithful with little, He knows He can trust you with more (Luke 16:10).

A healthy church environment can help form your purpose. It's where your calling can be confirmed and commissioned, where spiritual gifts are nurtured and where leaders are launched. We're building God's kingdom and kingdom people don't just sit where it's easy. They're open to God's leading and faithful wherever they're sent.

The Church Commissions Purpose

One of the clearest examples of this happens in Acts 13. The early church in Antioch is worshiping and praying when the Holy Spirit speaks:

"Set apart for me Barnabas and Saul for the work to which I have called them" (Acts 13:2).

What happens next?

"So after they had fasted and prayed, they placed their hands on them and sent them off" (Acts 13:3).

Barnabas and Paul didn't launch into their purpose independently. They were called out in community, affirmed by leadership and sent with *spiritual authority.* The church recognized what God had already placed in them. Through covering, prayer and relationship, they were released to walk in it.

That's still the model. Purpose and calling are not self-appointed. They are God-given gifts that are discovered and developed not on our own, but in the presence of community and healthy spiritual leadership.

Every believer has a ministry. That doesn't mean everyone will hold a microphone or have a full-time job at a church, but everyone has influence, gifts and a role. Being "set apart" and "sent" may look a little different for every person, depending on their calling and God's plan for their life. Being "sent" out into your purpose may not be overseas to be a missionary, but it might mean stepping up to lead a team in an area of church you might never have expected. It comes down to having a willing heart, being under a healthy spiritual covering and being faithful over time.

Pastor and author Eugene Peterson wrote a book called *A Long Obedience in the Same Direction.* I think the title alone is such a good representation of how purpose unfolds in our lives as we experience the richness of what God intends His children to experience. But it isn't easy. Peterson writes in the book, "There is a great market for religious experience in our world; there is little enthusiasm for the patient acquisition of virtue, little inclination to sign up for a long apprenticeship in what earlier generations of Christians called holiness."[2] Faithfulness comes before fulfillment. Purpose is about far more than what we can accomplish for God; it's also about what He wants to do in us.

Being planted in a church helps you discover your gifts, develop your character and deploy your purpose.

"Being confident of this, that he who began a good work in you will carry it on to completion until the day of Christ Jesus" (Philippians 1:6).

There's a critical shift when you realize that purpose isn't just about you. You're living a missional life.

"Therefore go and make disciples of all nations..." (Matthew 28:19).

Jesus didn't just call us to discover who we are. He called us to go into the world and make a difference. That mission doesn't begin on the mission field. It begins in your world.

The Word Is in the House

So often, the answer to your questions, the confirmation you've been seeking or the encouragement to take the next step is already in the mouth of someone in your small group or a leader in your church or your pastor. This is why remaining planted matters—because you need to be *in the room* to receive it. Proximity releases purpose. You never know which Sunday, which message, which conversation will unlock something God has been growing inside of you for years.

God could use a sermon to stir your calling. He could use a prayer moment to clarify your next step. He could use a lobby conversation to give you the courage to go.

But you have to be present to receive it.

Legacy Starts With "Yes"

Many people want to do something big for God, but everything big starts small.

A "yes" to serve. A "yes" to lead a small group. A "yes" to give. A "yes" to build someone else's vision while God shapes your own. That's how legacy begins.

"For this reason I remind you to fan into flame the gift of God, which is in you..." (2 Timothy 1:6).

You have a gift. A calling. A destiny. But it needs to be

stirred and fanned into flame. God begins to multiply your life in ways you never imagined when you serve faithfully, grow consistently, submit humbly and love deeply.

Your purpose is to know God personally and intimately and help others do the same. The calling God has for you will always involve impacting people. That's legacy. That's purpose. That's what the church is all about.

We're not called to sit; we're called to serve.

We're not called to consume; we're called to contribute.

We're not called to make a name for ourselves; we're called to make disciples for Jesus.

You're Not Done Yet

For some people, purpose isn't a mystery anymore. You've built a career. You've raised a family. You've achieved more than you once thought possible. You've developed skills, influence and leadership instincts that others admire. In many ways, you're operating in your purpose every day. But let me encourage you with something: **you're not done yet.**

You haven't peaked spiritually. You haven't exhausted your usefulness in the kingdom. You haven't already given the best of what you have to offer. In fact, some of the most important impact God wants to bring through your life may still be ahead of you. It won't happen in a boardroom, on a project or in the marketplace. It will happen in God's House.

The local church needs people like you. People with maturity, stability, leadership instincts and real-world experience. You bring a perspective that younger believers don't have yet. You carry wisdom gained through wins and losses. You understand commitment. You understand sacrifice. And whether you realize it or not, people in your church are hungry for someone just like you to step into their world.

"Even in old age they will still produce fruit; they will remain vital and green" (Psalm 92:14 NLT).

This isn't about age. It's about readiness. Staying "vital and green" means your life is still producing, still influencing, still multiplying beyond the walls of your career.

You may feel like: *I'm already making a difference. My plate is already full. I don't really have a role at church.*

But here's the truth: **Success in the world doesn't replace significance in the kingdom.**

Your church doesn't need you to quit your job or change careers. It simply needs you to bring what you already carry into the environment where God shapes people for eternity.

Practically, this could look like:

- Taking a younger man or woman under your wing.
- Serving as a team leader and modeling excellence.
- Helping strengthen a ministry with your operational or leadership gifting.
- Hosting a small group and pouring into couples, parents or young professionals.
- Being a steady, consistent presence that your pastor can rely on.
- Helping new believers navigate the real-world challenges of following Jesus.

These aren't "extra" things. They are kingdom things that only people like you can do. *"For everyone to whom much is given, from him much will be required..."* (Luke 12:48 NKJV).

This isn't pressure. It is purpose. You are not on the sidelines of the story God is writing in your church. You are one of the people He is counting on to help shape it. Your leadership matters. Your presence matters. Your voice matters. Your example matters. And your church needs the best of what you carry, right now.

You're not done yet. Not even close. The next stretch of impact in your life may be the most meaningful one, not because it builds your resumé, but because it builds God's House.

God's Purpose Is Bigger Than You

You may not see the full picture now or feel like your role is small, that your impact is hidden. Like your "yes" doesn't matter. But that's not true. Every small act of faithfulness is part of a bigger plan. Remember, our faithfulness lays the foundation for fulfillment. Our part is to be faithful; God's part is the fulfillment. We may be tempted to try to bring about the fulfillment of our purpose in our own way and on our own timeline, but faithfulness is the best investment you can make when it comes to fulfilling your purpose. When we do our part—nothing more, nothing less—then we are allowing God to do His part. And He will always fulfill His purpose for our lives better than we ever could.

In Psalm 138:8 (ESV), David says, *"The Lord will fulfill*

his purpose for me; your steadfast love, O Lord, endures forever..."

You can be confident of this: God wants good things for you, even more than you want them for yourself. He has a plan and a purpose for your life. You are part of something bigger than yourself and it is unfolding, piece by piece, day by day, in the House of God where you are planted.

Action Steps

If you want to walk in God's unfolding purpose, here are a few steps to take:

- **Find a spiritual leader/mentor who can help you grow.** Invite their feedback and insight into your life. Ask where you can grow and be willing to hear from them and learn with a humble heart.

- **Say "yes" to stretch moments.** When you're asked to lead, to step up, to go beyond what feels comfortable, don't write it off. Be willing to consider things that may feel uncomfortable. We may not always feel ready or equipped, and it may not always feel convenient, but some of the greatest growth comes through saying yes to uncomfortable opportunities that stretch us.

- **Help someone else grow. One of the most powerful things we can do is invest in people and invest in building God's kingdom through the local church.** Legacy isn't about making a name for ourselves. It's about investing our effort, time and energy into something that will impact others for eternity. Who are you raising up? Who are you helping mentor and grow? Whose life is being impacted by yours?

Reflection Questions

1. In what ways has the local church helped shape your understanding of purpose?

2. What's one area where you feel called to lead, serve or stretch, but maybe haven't said yes to yet?

3. Who can you begin encouraging or investing in as part of your legacy?

GRACED FOR A PLACE

GRACED FOR A PLACE

"The one thing I ask of the Lord—the thing I seek most—is to live in the house of the Lord all the days of my life, delighting in the Lord's perfections and meditating in his Temple" (Psalm 27:4 NLT).

Some places just stay with you. I can think of several in my own life that marked me in lasting ways. Maybe for you, it's the house you grew up in, the spot where you said "yes" to your spouse, a classroom, a hospital room or a quiet space where you first felt God speak to your heart. We all have places that shape us—some filled with joy, others with pain. But all of them leave an imprint.

That's because environments matter. People and places matter. God designed it that way. The environments we're in shape who we become, and they are a big part of how God works in our lives.

God Calls Us to People and Places

Throughout Scripture, we see a consistent pattern: God calls His people into *specific* places for *specific* purposes. Throughout the Bible, we see that God calls people into location-specific assignments:

- God placed Adam and Eve in a garden.
- God called Abraham to leave one land and go to another.

- God brought Israel to the Promised Land.
- God gave Moses instructions for the Tabernacle.
- God filled Solomon's Temple with His Presence.
- God moved the early Christians from city to city in the Book of Acts.

From the beginning, God has been intentional with location. He knows that *where* we are shapes *who* we become and what we can accomplish.

There Is Purpose in the Place

One of my favorite stories about "place" comes from the Old Testament Book of Genesis. In Genesis 28, Jacob is on a journey that his father Isaac has sent him on. Along the way, Jacob stops for the night and he has a divine encounter that redefines everything in his life.

"...Surely the Lord is in this place, and I was not aware of it" (Genesis 28:16).

That one moment led him to say: *"...How awesome is this place! This is none other than the house of God; this is the gate of heaven"* (Genesis 28:17).

Some places are more than locations. They're assignments. Environments. Places where God speaks, shapes and sends.

And I think it's important to point out that what led Jacob to that specific place flowed out of his relationship with a person. Sometimes, we have those transformative experiences with God while we're simply being obedient to take the next step or being faithful to the process. It may not start out glamorous. Obedience and faithfulness often aren't. And we may not even have full clarity on what God is doing or calling us to. That's okay. Stay faithful to the process and follow your next step. Just like God met Jacob on his journey, He will meet you on yours, too. Something supernatural takes place when we have a willing heart, we're aligned with the right people and we're going to the right places.

The where of your life is deeply connected to the what of your purpose. There are many places where we could choose to plant our lives—to put down roots, invest our time and allow the culture and community around us to shape us. But Scripture is clear:

"... planted ***in the house of the Lord,*** *they will flourish* ***in the courts of our God****"*
(Psalm 92:13, emphasis mine).

The righteous flourish because they're planted in a specific place, under God's design. You can't separate purpose from placement. And when you find the place God has graced you for, you don't just grow—you *flourish*.

What Does It Look Like to Be Graced for a Place?

I think it's important to know that being graced for a place starts with finding the right posture for your heart. We do the right things, but if our heart isn't in it and it's just performative, we're going to miss out on the full experience God is inviting us into.

Do our actions matter? Of course. But while humans look at the external, God looks at the internal (1 Samuel 16:7). He is always most concerned with the state of our heart, and when it comes to this area, humility is one of the most important postures our heart needs to carry.

In James 4:6, the Bible tells us that, *"God resists the proud, But gives grace to the humble"* (NKJV). It's hard to be graced for something if we have pride standing in the way. If we're carrying a stubborn, resistant posture of the heart or if we're holding certain parts of our lives back from God's reach, we're blocking His grace and favor.

On the other hand, a soft, humble, flexible heart is

a magnet for God's grace and favor. This posture allows us to receive the grace He wants to give us for the journey He's called us to. There's a willingness in people who are in the flow of God's grace. They serve with joy. They stay with maturity. They give with vision. They grow with consistency. They lead with humility. They carry a spirit that values belonging and responsibility. Their language sounds like:

How can I help build this?

What's needed here?

Who can I encourage today?

That's what happens when you know that you've been graced for a place. When you know God has called you to a church, you expand your focus from simply asking, *How can the church invest in my life?* to thinking that sounds more like this: *I know that being planted in this church is going to build my life; how can I also invest in the church and help make a difference in others' lives?* That shift from just receiving to investing is one of the most important transformations in a believer's life. It moves us from simply being impacted to creating impact that will last for eternity.

The Power of God's Presence

There's something you sense when you walk into a healthy church. Peace. Purpose. Joy. Honor. Expectation. Healing. Strength.

The presence of God is not confined to buildings, but it is often cultivated in environments where people are unified, planted and surrendered.

"Lord, I love the house where you live, the place where your glory dwells" (Psalm 26:8).

"Blessed are those you choose and bring near to live in your courts! We are filled with the good things of your house..." (Psalm 65:4).

When you walk into God's House, you're stepping into an atmosphere that changes things. An atmosphere of faith. An atmosphere of clarity. An atmosphere of vision. An atmosphere of restoration. God's presence should always be the defining force in a church's atmosphere. But God also gives us a part to play. We help set the tone for what others experience when they walk in—from what they see, to how they're welcomed, to how they get connected and the list goes on. When you think about the lives that are changed as people find hope, freedom, healing and restoration, it gives perspective on what we get to be a part of. What an honor to get to be a part of someone's sacred journey to knowing God and experiencing His work in their life!

When you're graced for a place, you don't just benefit from that atmosphere. You help create it. As a result, you're part of a kingdom endeavor that has lasting, eternal impact. Not only is that an incredible gift and a privilege to be a part of. It's what we were made for.

A Heart That Honors God's House

All throughout Scripture, we see God's deep love for His House. From the detailed blueprints He gave Moses for the Tabernacle, to the beauty and excellence that marked Solomon's Temple, we see God's care and attention to the details. When Jesus entered the Temple courts and saw people who claimed to be doing God's work extorting the vulnerable and using His House for their own financial gain, He didn't walk in quietly. He quickly and passionately spoke up and drove out what didn't belong and what didn't reflect God's heart.

In the Book of Haggai, when God's people were neglecting God's House, He made it clear that their priorities weren't in alignment:

"'Go up into the mountains and bring down timber and build my house, so that I may take pleasure in it and be honored,' says the Lord. 'You expected much, but see, it turned out to be little'... 'Because of my house, which remains a ruin, while each of you is busy with your own house'" (Haggai 1:8–9).

God was confronting His people because they were building their personal lives while neglecting His House. He wasn't against them building their own homes, but He was calling them back to first things first. If we put God first, He takes care of us.

That's what happens when we honor the House of God. We're not just maintaining a building or fulfilling a duty. We're creating a place for His presence to dwell and for lives to be changed. When we pour our time, our prayers and our hearts into His Church, we get to be part of the very thing that matters so much to God.

It's not about obligation; it's about opportunity. It's about loving what He loves. It's about saying, *Lord, I want to build what You're building.*

When you've discovered the place God has graced you for, you start to see His House not as something you attend but something you belong to. You begin to carry His heart for it. His House matters to you because you love the One who dwells there.

Excellence Honors God

We're building a home for His presence. That's why excellence matters. Excellence demonstrates, *God, You're worth my best.*

In the Book of Malachi, God begins by expressing His deep love for His people: *"'I have loved you,' says the Lord"* (Malachi 1:2). Yet through the prophet, He shows them that their worship no longer reflects that same love. They had grown casual, offering what was convenient and treating holy things as common. They had lost the sense of reverence and honor that should mark genuine love. He was calling them back to the kind of relationship where love looks like honor, where devotion is visible in how we serve, give and bring our best.

That same invitation is extended to us. When we serve, give, lead or create with excellence, we reflect His nature and His heart. We honor Him by preparing well, leading with care and giving with joy.

Excellence looks like:

- Being well-prepared.
- Leading with character and wisdom.
- Serving with consistency and joy.
- Going the extra mile to do things well.
- Giving faithfully and with a generous, faith-filled heart.
- Loving people well—seeing them as made in the image of God and treating them with genuine care and concern.

This doesn't mean perfection. It means *intention* and doing the best you can with what you have. Doing everything as if you were doing it for Him, because you are.

"Whatever you do, work at it with all your heart, as working for the Lord..." (Colossians 3:23).

Excellence creates an atmosphere where people can meet with God, and it's one of the most tangible ways we live out what it means to be "graced for a place."

Build What Jesus Is Building

Think back to that bold declaration Jesus spoke: *"...I will build my church, and the gates of Hades will not overcome it"* (Matthew 16:18).

This is what Jesus is building, and as believers, we're called to build the church too. It's the one place we know that our investment of our effort and energy will last for eternity. Everything else only has temporal value.

"Unless the Lord builds the house, the builders labor in vain" (Psalm 127:1).

You're not just called to attend. You're not just called to benefit. You're called to build. We don't serve because we have to; we serve because we get to.

This doesn't mean you're always only pouring out, never receiving. It doesn't mean you'll never have needs. It doesn't mean church isn't a place of healing and help for your own life. Being a mature believer who is committed to God's House means it's not just about us anymore. Instead, it's about knowing that the local church is the hope of the world, and each of us has a part to play in its story.

Practical Ways to Build the House

If you're wondering what this looks like in everyday life, here are some practical ways to invest in and build your local church.

1. **Serve on a team.** Whether it's greeting at the door, leading worship, helping with kids or running production—your gifts matter.

2. **Give consistently and sacrificially.** Generosity isn't just about funding the vision. It's about faith and obedience.

3. **Show up early, stay late.** Create margin to encourage someone, meet a new guest or pray with a friend.

4. **Invite others.** Don't keep it to yourself. Extend the grace you've received to those who need it.

5. **Protect the unity.** Speak well of your church. Shut down gossip. Choose encouragement over critique.

6. **Pray for your pastors and leaders.** Cover them with faith. Your prayers make a difference.

If You Build His House, He'll Build Yours

One of the greatest promises in Scripture is this: when you prioritize God's House, He takes care of yours.

"Seek first the kingdom of God and his righteousness, and all these things will be added to you" (Matthew 6:33 ESV).

This doesn't mean everything becomes easy, but it does mean you'll have God's hand on your life. I've seen it time and time again. People who were struggling (emotionally, financially, relationally) decided to lean in to what the Word says and get planted and devote themselves to the House of God. They served. They gave. They put down roots and stayed faithful, even when it wasn't easy. God began to restore and rebuild their lives in ways they never expected. That shouldn't be our motivation, but it is the blessing that comes when we're faithful.

Your Legacy Starts Here

Legacy doesn't begin someday in the future. Legacy begins with what you're devoting your time, effort and energy to right now. Are the things you're investing in now going to build a life that leaves the legacy you desire? A legacy that honors God and reflects a life devoted to things that really matter?

Legacy starts today, and we get to choose what kind of legacy we leave. Every prayer, every act of service, every offering, every word of encouragement—it's all part of something that will outlast us.

"A good person leaves an inheritance for their children's children..." (Proverbs 13:22).

"This is to my Father's glory, that you bear much fruit..." (John 15:8).

You're holding the baton of faith in your generation.

So the question becomes:

What kind of church will you help build?

What kind of spiritual home will you leave behind?

What kind of legacy will your family remember?

Because when you're graced for a place and committed to building God's House, you're not just making a difference for today. You're shaping eternity.

Closing Action Steps

To finish this journey strong, here's what I challenge you to do:

- **Go all in.** Stop waiting for a sign. Start moving with faith. Plant yourself in God's House and don't look back.

- **Find your place.** Ask a pastor or leader where you're needed. Look for open doors and then step through them.

- **Build with vision.** Give. Serve. Stay. Multiply. Invest your life where God has placed you.

- **Stay planted.** Don't uproot in the hard seasons. There's grace for this place. Trust God's timing and stay faithful. When we do our part, He is always faithful to do His. His plans are far better than any we could create for ourselves.

Final Reflection Questions

1. What might God be calling you to do that could make an impact for eternity? What places might you need to surrender to God and say, *Here are my gifts and talents, Lord. Use them as you will*?

2. What would it look like for you to fully embrace your place in your local church?

3. What legacy do you hope to leave through your investment in God's House?

And with that...

Welcome Home.

NOTES

God's House, God's Idea

1. Eugene H. Peterson, *The Pastor: A Memoir* (New York: HarperOne, 2011).

God's Unfolding Purpose

2. Eugene H. Peterson, *A Long Obedience in the Same Direction* (Downers Grove, IL: InterVarsity Press, 1980).

ABOUT THE AUTHOR

John Siebeling and his wife Leslie are the founding and senior pastors of The Life Church, based in Memphis, Tennessee—a thriving, multi-campus church with locations throughout the United States and internationally with a diverse body of believers committed to serving people, developing leaders and impacting generations. John's passion for other cultures began as a missionary in Nairobi, Kenya. While serving on the pastoral staff of Nairobi Lighthouse Church, God stirred his heart to return to the States and build a diverse, life-giving church.

Though most of his time and energy remain focused on pastoring The Life Church, John also speaks for many incredible ministries and organizations, and coaches a network of pastors and churches. He is the founder of Make Room, a ministry designed to help pastors and leaders build the church. Today, Make Room hosts conferences on four continents and serves thousands of pastors. John also serves as a founding board member of the Association of Related Churches and is the author of several books focused on helping people experience God's best and move forward in life.

For more information about John Siebeling and The Life Church, visit johnsiebeling.com or connect with @johnsiebeling on Instagram.

TAKE ANOTHER STEP
IN YOUR WALK WITH GOD.